Hello! 200 300-Calorie Pasta Recipes

(300-Calorie Pasta Recipes - Volume 1)

Best 300-Calorie Pasta Cookbook Ever For Beginners

Ms. Pasta

Content

Introduction

***

Hi all,

Welcome to MrandMsCooking.com — a website created by a community of cooking enthusiasts with the goal of providing books for novice cooks featuring the best recipes, at the most affordable prices, and valuable gifts.

Before we go to the pasta recipes in the book "Hello! 200 300-Calorie Pasta Recipes", I have an interesting story to share with you about how I learned about pasta.

In Vietnam, pasta began to be served in restaurants about 7 to 8 years ago and quickly became a trendy, high-end and Western priced dish. However, my mother cooked the first pasta dish I ever ate, not a fancy restaurant. While my sister and I were still in school, we heard about the so-called Spaghetti from the press and friends, but we didn't think of trying it. My parent, who were state employees, had a hard enough time keeping us clothed, putting food on the table and getting us educated to think about eating such fancy food. That is why eating "luxurious" dishes such as Spaghetti is not one of our main priorities of attention and care.

Coming home from school one evening, my mother told us that we will have Spaghetti for dinner. We were very happy and surprised about this and thought there is something special to celebrate, but we learned that she got the recipe from some friends, then bought the needed ingredients and prepared the dish. She concluded that: "I was very keen to know how special the spaghetti is, but it is really simple, just like Vietnamese fried noodles." If the other dishes prepared by my mother are special, I can say that this noodle is much more special. Because my mother is generally unfamiliar with Western things, like she has just learned how to order pizza only recently and the name still confuses her: "What is the name of that round cake with different ingredients on it, does it start with the letter "P" or letter "B"?", that is why it is very surprising that learn that she knows about Spaghetti and was able to cook it with right ingredients. Her first version of noodles was a twist on fried noodles, stirred with tomatoes and some vegetables, it had no cream, Parmesan or any other Italian spices. It was very different from the traditional pasta, but it was actually very delicious.

Pasta these days is available almost everywhere and no longer considered a high-end dish. You can enjoy spaghetti anytime you want, and I have tried it in well-known restaurants, even in its homeland, but my mother's first pasta plate will always be the best. It is so memorable because it is the first time and you know it is the best because no other pasta will be cooked with such motherly love.

With that first pasta plate, overflowing with all my mother's love, I have come to love pasta and learn more about it. Learning about pasta has taught me many interesting things and about different dishes. Spaghetti is one of the popular pasta names out there but there are more kinds and I will be sharing them with you in the next parts. I wrote this book out of my passion and love for you. In this series about pasta recipes, there are other topics too such as:

- Homemade Pasta Recipes
- Pasta By Shape Recipes
- Pasta Salad Recipes
- ...

You have reached the end of the article. Thank you for your support and for choosing "Hello! 200 300-Calorie Pasta Recipes". Let this be an inspiration when preparing food in your kitchen. Please tell us your pasta story in the comment sections below.

List of Abbreviations

CᴏᴏKing	
LIST OF ABBREVIATIONS	
tbsp(s).	tablespoon(s)
tsp(s).	teaspoon(s)
c.	cup(s)
oz.	ounce(s)
lb(s).	pound(s)

200 Amazing 300 Calorie Pasta Recipes

***

1. 3-cheese Eggplant Lasagna

""Come up with your own taste by measuring and adjusting the spices depending on your likings. The ingredients of this recipe have a lot of vegetables, so it's healthy.""

Serving: 8 | Prep: 40m | Ready in: 2h25m

Ingredients

- 2 eggplants, sliced lengthwise into 1/4-inch thick slices
- 2 tbsps. salt
- 2 tbsps. canola oil
- 1 (28 oz.) can crushed tomatoes
- 1 (6 oz.) can tomato paste
- 1 tsp. dried oregano
- 1 tsp. dried basil
- 1 tsp. garlic powder
- 1 tsp. onion powder
- 1 tbsp. olive oil
- salt and ground black pepper to taste
- 1 tsp. olive oil
- 1 onion, diced
- 1 cup frozen chopped spinach
- 1 cup shredded carrot
- 1 (15 oz.) container ricotta cheese
- 2 eggs
- 1/2 cup freshly grated Romano cheese
- 1 tsp. garlic powder
- 1 tsp. onion powder
- 1/2 tsp. salt
- 1 cup shredded mozzarella cheese

Direction

- Get 2 tbsp. of salt and sprinkle it on the sides of eggplant slices. Arrange them in a large baking pan placing paper towels on every layer.
- On top of the eggplant slices, put a smaller baking pan and weigh it down with some food cans. Allow it to sit for about 60 minutes or more until you observed that the paper towels are moist.
- Wash the sliced eggplant with freshwater and pat dry it using paper towels.
- Spread 2 tbsp. of canola oil on a heated large pan.
- Cook the sides of eggplant slices for about 5 mins per side until it turns slightly brown. You can cook by batches if needed. Set it aside after cooking.
- In another bowl, mix oregano, 1 tsp. of garlic powder, crushed tomatoes, basil, 1 tsp. of onion powder, salt, black pepper, tomato paste and 1 tbsp. of olive oil. Set aside for a while.
- Prepare a pan and heat 1 tsp. of olive oil over a medium heat. Let it cook for about 5 minutes until it looks transparent.
- Mix in shredded carrots and the frozen spinach. Wait for about 5-8 minutes for it to cook and dry the mixture. Let it cool when done.
- In a separate bowl, mix Romano cheese, 1 tsp. of garlic powder, half tsp. of salt, eggs, ricotta cheese and 1 tsp. of onion powder.
- Transfer the cooled mixture of spinach and carrot into the ricotta mixture and mix.
- Set your oven at 350°F (175°C) for preheating.
- To assemble the lasagna, prepare first a 9x13-inch baking pan and spread thin layer of tomato sauce in it.

- Top the tomato sauce with half of the eggplant slices and arrange in a layer.
- On top of the eggplant layer, pour half of the ricotta cheese mixture.
- Spread another layer of the tomato sauce and arrange again the remaining slices of eggplant and the mixture of ricotta (same with the previous step).
- End the layer with a tomato sauce and top it with mozzarella cheese.
- Let it bake in the preheated oven for 45 mins. until the cheese turns to brown. Allow it to sit for 10 minutes. Serve.

Nutrition Information

- Calories: 285 calories;
- Total Carbohydrate: 20.8 g
- Cholesterol: 80 mg
- Total Fat: 16 g
- Protein: 17.3 g
- Sodium: 2475 mg

2. Al's Quick Vegetarian Spaghetti

"It has no meat."
Serving: 8 | Prep: 10m | Ready in: 30m

Ingredients

- 1 lb. uncooked spaghetti
- 1 cup broccoli florets
- 1 (15 oz.) can whole kernel corn, drained
- 1 cup fresh sliced mushrooms
- 1 cup sliced carrots
- 2 (8 oz.) cans tomato sauce

Direction

- Boil the salted water in a large pot. Put in spaghetti and bring water back to a boil. Cook until the spaghetti is al dente, then drain well.
- In large sauce pot, combine tomato sauce, carrots, mushrooms, corn and broccoli. Cook on medium heat until vegetables become tender or for 15-20 mins. Prevent the sauce from sticking by stirring occasionally. Add sauce over the spaghetti. Enjoy!

Nutrition Information

- Calories: 279 calories;
- Total Carbohydrate: 57.8 g
- Cholesterol: 0 mg
- Total Fat: 1.6 g
- Protein: 10.3 g
- Sodium: 468 mg

3. Alfredo Light

"Sometimes I use peas for broccoli."
Serving: 8 | Prep: 20m | Ready in: 40m

Ingredients

- 1 onion, chopped
- 1 clove garlic, minced
- 2 tsps. vegetable oil
- 2 cups skim milk
- 1 cup chicken broth
- 3 tbsps. all-purpose flour
- 1/2 tsp. salt
- 1/4 tsp. ground black pepper
- 1/2 cup grated Parmesan cheese
- 16 oz. dry fettuccine pasta
- 1 (16 oz.) package frozen broccoli florets

Direction

- Heat oil in medium saucepan on medium heat. Add garlic and onion; sauté till golden brown.
- Mix pepper, salt, flour, chicken broth and milk in small saucepan on low heat till thick and smooth; mix into onion mixture. Cook on medium low heat till sauce is thick, frequently mix. Mix Parmesan cheese in.
- Meanwhile, in boiling water, cook pasta. At final few minutes of cooking, add broccoli to pasta; cook till pasta is al dente.
- Drain veggies and pasta; put in big bowl, then toss with sauce and serve.

Nutrition Information

- Calories: 292 calories;
- Total Carbohydrate: 50.5 g
- Cholesterol: 6 mg
- Total Fat: 4.1 g
- Protein: 13.9 g
- Sodium: 360 mg

4. All Natural Ramen Noodles

"Super simple!"
Serving: 4 | Prep: 10m | Ready in: 20m

Ingredients

- 4 cups vegetable broth
- 4 cups water
- 1 tbsp. soy sauce
- 1 tbsp. sesame oil
- 1 tbsp. ground ginger
- 1 tbsp. Sriracha hot sauce
- 9 oz. soba noodles

Direction

- In a pot, combine hot sauce, ginger, sesame oil, soy sauce, water and broth. Boil. Put noodles into the boiling broth mixture. Cook for 5-7 mins until the noodles become tender but still firm to the bite. Place the noodles into the serving bowls. Pour the preferred amount of the broth on top.

Nutrition Information

- Calories: 280 calories;
- Total Carbohydrate: 53.6 g
- Cholesterol: 0 mg
- Total Fat: 4.4 g
- Protein: 10.4 g
- Sodium: 1351 mg

5. American Chop Suey

"This dish is so hearty."
Serving: 8 | Prep: 5m | Ready in: 20m

Ingredients

- 1 lb. lean ground beef
- 1/2 cup chopped celery
- 1/2 cup chopped onion
- 1 (14.5 oz.) can stewed tomatoes
- 2 (15 oz.) cans spaghetti with sauce

Direction

- Brown beef in large skillet with onion and celery until the onion becomes tender. Put in spaghetti and tomatoes. Heat while stirring all together. Enjoy with the garlic bread, and if desired, a dinner salad.

Nutrition Information

- Calories: 249 calories;
- Total Carbohydrate: 20.7 g
- Cholesterol: 46 mg
- Total Fat: 12.5 g
- Protein: 13 g
- Sodium: 565 mg

6. Angel Hair Pasta Chicken

"You family will adore this dish."
Serving: 6 | Prep: 10m | Ready in: 30m

Ingredients

- 2 tbsps. olive oil, divided
- 2 skinless, boneless chicken breast halves - cubed
- 12 oz. angel hair pasta
- 1 carrot, sliced diagonally into 1/4 inch thick slices
- 1 (10 oz.) package frozen broccoli florets, thawed
- 2 cloves garlic, minced
- 2/3 cup chicken broth

- 1 tsp. dried basil
- 1/4 cup grated Parmesan cheese

Direction

- Over medium heat, heat 1 tbsps. of oil in a medium skillet. Put chicken and sauté until chicken is no longer pink or cooked through for 5 to 7 minutes. Take it out from the skillet and let it drain on paper towels.
- In a big pot, let lightly salted water boil. Put pasta and cook until al dente or for 2 to 4 minutes. Drain it and set aside.
- In the same skillet used for the chicken, heat 2nd tbsp. of oil over medium heat while pasta is cooking. For 4 minutes, stir fry carrots. Put garlic and broccoli and for another 2 minutes, continue stir frying. Lastly, stir in cheese, basil and broth and put the chicken back to the skillet. Turn heat to low and for 4 minute, let it simmer.
- In a big serving bowl, put drained pasta. Put vegetable or chicken mixture on top. Immediately serve.

Nutrition Information

- Calories: 280 calories;
- Total Carbohydrate: 34.6 g
- Cholesterol: 27 mg
- Total Fat: 8.3 g
- Protein: 17.5 g
- Sodium: 200 mg

7. Angel Hair Pasta With Peppers And Chicken

"It not only looks pretty but also tastes great!"
Serving: 8

Ingredients

- 1 tsp. olive oil
- 1 tbsp. minced garlic
- 1 large red bell pepper, julienned
- 3/4 (8 oz.) can sliced water chestnuts

- 1 cup sugar snap pea pods
- 6 thick slices smoked deli chicken
- 1 tbsp. onion powder
- 1/4 tsp. ground black pepper
- 1 pinch salt
- 1 cup chicken broth
- 2 (8 oz.) packages angel hair pasta

Direction

- Heat olive oil in large skillet to medium high heat. Put in pea pods, water chestnuts, bell pepper and garlic. Lower the heat to medium low. Cook, covered, for 5 mins.
- Cut the chicken into roughly 1/4-inch-wide strips. Put salt, ground black pepper, onion powder and chicken into skillet. Cook, covered, for 5 mins longer.
- Heat chicken broth in separate small saucepan to a near boil. Pour hot broth to chicken/vegetable pan. Toss, then add the mixture over the cooked angel hair pasta immediately. Serve.

Nutrition Information

- Calories: 222 calories;
- Total Carbohydrate: 38.2 g
- Cholesterol: 10 mg
- Total Fat: 2.8 g
- Protein: 10.7 g
- Sodium: 369 mg

8. Angel's Pasta

"This dish is a light and delicate vegetarian pasta."
Serving: 6 | Prep: 10m | Ready in: 25m

Ingredients

- 8 oz. angel hair pasta
- 1 tbsp. crushed garlic
- 1 tbsp. olive oil
- 2 zucchini, sliced
- salt and pepper to taste
- 3 tomatoes, chopped

- 12 leaves fresh basil
- 4 oz. mozzarella cheese, shredded

Direction

- In a big pot, let lightly salted water boil. Put pasta and cook until al dente or for 8 to 10 minutes. Drain.
- Meanwhile, over medium heat, heat a medium skillet. Put in oil and sauté the garlic until it turns golden in color. Stir in pepper, salt and zucchini. Sauté for 2 minutes and put in tomato. Wait for a few minutes more to cook. Before mixing with pasta, chop basil and put into vegetables.
- Mix vegetables and pasta. Put mozzarella on top and serve.

Nutrition Information

- Calories: 201 calories;
- Total Carbohydrate: 26.9 g
- Cholesterol: 12 mg
- Total Fat: 6.6 g
- Protein: 10.1 g
- Sodium: 202 mg

9. Anna's German Dumplings

"Let's cook a wonderful meal!"
Serving: 12 | Prep: 15m | Ready in: 1h35m

Ingredients

- 3/4 cup milk
- 1/2 tsp. salt
- 1 1/2 tbsps. all-purpose flour
- 1/2 cup cold water
- 1 cup all-purpose flour
- 3 eggs, beaten
- 1 cup all-purpose flour

Direction

- In a saucepan over medium heat, put salt and milk. Mix water and 1 1/2 tbsps. flour together in small bowl. Stir in flour mixture when milk

starts to bubble; cook for 2-3 mins until thickened, stirring constantly. Allow to cool till it set. You can place mixture in fridge to speed the process.

- Fold eggs into chilled dough. Put in one cup of the flour; mix thoroughly (the dough will become lumpy). Drop by teaspoonful into the simmering soups. Cover and simmer for 10 mins. Take off the lid, simmer for 10 more mins.

Nutrition Information

- Calories: 108 calories;
- Total Carbohydrate: 17.6 g
- Cholesterol: 36 mg
- Total Fat: 2 g
- Protein: 4.1 g
- Sodium: 122 mg

10. Babaci's Potato Pierogi

"A Polish recipe handed down from the family."
Serving: 24 | Prep: 1h | Ready in: 1h30m

Ingredients

- 12 Yukon Gold potatoes, peeled and quartered
- 3 eggs
- 3 tbsps. cream cheese, divided
- 3 tsps. milk, divided
- 2 cups all-purpose flour, divided
- 2 1/2 (8 oz.) containers cottage cheese
- salt to taste
- 2 tbsps. butter
- oil for frying

Direction

- Boil a big pot of salted water, the add potatoes. Cook it for about 15 minutes until it becomes soft yet still firm. Drain it and let it cool.
- Prepare the dough by mixing 1/2 cup of flour, 1 tsp. of milk, 1 tbsp. of cream cheese and 1 egg. When all the flour has been incorporated, add additional 1 tsp. of milk, 1 tbsp. of cream cheese and 1/2 cup of flour. Once the dough is

well incorporated, add another 1/2 cup of flour, 1 tbsp. of cream cheese and 1 egg, then combine well. Lastly, add the leftover egg, 1/2 cup of flour and 1 tsp. of milk. If the mixture is too wet, add more flour, but if the mixture is too dry, add a bit of milk.

- Roll out the 1/4 of the dough into 1/4-inch thick onto a well-floured surface. Cut out circles form the dough using a muffin cutter, glass or any rounded surface. Put flour on each side of the circle and arrange in one layer on a wax paper. Redo the process with the leftover dough.
- Mash the potatoes with butter, salt and cottage cheese. Slightly below the middle of the dough circle, put a spoonful of the filling, then fold the dough over and with your fingertips, secure the edges. You have to stretch the dough over so you have to put enough filling; do not put so much as it might squeeze out when the dough is sealed.
- Boil a big pot of salted water then drop in the pierogis, a few pieces at a time. Cook until they float to the top, or for 1-2 minutes. Drain it.
- In a big pan, heat the oil on medium-high heat then fry the boiled pierogis in hot oil until it becomes crispy.

Nutrition Information

- Calories: 201 calories;
- Total Carbohydrate: 27.9 g
- Cholesterol: 31 mg
- Total Fat: 7.1 g
- Protein: 6.6 g
- Sodium: 121 mg

11. Baked Pasta Primavera

"A great dish for summer."
Serving: 8 | Prep: 25m | Ready in: 45m

Ingredients

- Reynolds Wrap® Pan Lining Paper
- 8 oz. dried fettuccine or linguine pasta
- 1 cup shredded carrots*
- 1 cup fresh or frozen peas
- 1 cup sliced yellow squash
- 1 cup fresh asparagus spears, cut into 1-inch pieces
- 2 tbsps. butter
- 2 tbsps. all-purpose flour
- 1/2 tsp. salt
- 1 cup lowfat milk
- 1/2 cup reduced-sodium chicken broth
- 4 oz. herbed goat cheese
- 1/2 cup cherry tomatoes, halved
- 1/2 cup grated Parmesan cheese, divided
- 1 tbsp. snipped fresh basil
- 1 tbsp. snipped fresh oregano
- 1/4 cup sliced almonds

Direction

- Preheat an oven to 400°F. Line Reynolds wrap Pan Lining Paper on 2-qt. rectangular baking dish, parchment side up; you don't need to grease the dish.
- Follow package directions to cook pasta in Dutch oven; at final 3 minutes of cooking time, add squash, asparagus, peas and/or carrots; drain. Keep 1/4 cup pasta water. Put pasta mixture in Dutch oven. Cover; put aside.
- Melt butter in medium saucepan; whisk salt and flour in. Whisk goat cheese, chicken broth and milk in; mix and cook on medium heat till bubbly and thick. Mix and cook for 1 minute; mix oregano, basil, 1/4 cup parmesan cheese, tomatoes and reserved pasta water in.
- Put milk mixture on pasta mixture; toss to coat. Put pasta mixture in prepped baking dish; sprinkle leftover 1/4 cup parmesan cheese and almonds.
- Bake till sauce is bubbly and mixture just begins to turn golden for 15-20 minutes.

Nutrition Information

- Calories: 269 calories;
- Total Carbohydrate: 30.2 g
- Cholesterol: 26 mg
- Total Fat: 11.5 g

- Protein: 12.5 g
- Sodium: 368 mg

12. Baked Shells In Sauce

"Easily adaptable and filling main dish."
Serving: 2 | Prep: 10m | Ready in: 40m

Ingredients

- 1/2 cup seashell pasta
- 1 cup tomato sauce
- 1/2 cup mushrooms, diced
- 1/4 cup crumbled firm silken tofu
- 1/4 cup shredded mozzarella cheese
- 2 tbsps. grated Parmesan cheese

Direction

- Boil a pot of slightly salted water. Put in the pasta and cook till al dente, about 8 to 10 minutes; drain.
- Preheat an oven to 200 °C or 400 °F.
- Mix tofu, mushrooms and tomato sauce in a medium bowl. Mix in the cooked pasta. Mix Parmesan cheeses and mozzarella in another small bowl.
- Arrange layers of pasta mixture and cheeses in a small casserole dish.
- In prepped oven, bake till slightly browned, about half an hour.

Nutrition Information

- Calories: 212 calories;
- Total Carbohydrate: 29.5 g
- Cholesterol: 13 mg
- Total Fat: 5.5 g
- Protein: 13.3 g
- Sodium: 819 mg

13. Baked Spaghetti Squash Lasagna Style

""This recipe is similar to Rigatoni and Lasagna. This would serve as a substitute to bland old spaghetti. Try making this and your kids will surely love this.""
Serving: 6 | Prep: 30m | Ready in: 1h45m

Ingredients

- 1 spaghetti squash, halved lengthwise and seeded
- 1 onion, chopped
- 2 tbsps. minced garlic
- 2 (14 oz.) cans stewed tomatoes
- 1 tbsp. dried basil
- 1 cube vegetable bouillon
- black pepper to taste
- 1 (15 oz.) can black olives, chopped
- 1 cup shredded mozzarella cheese
- 1 cup shredded Parmesan cheese

Direction

- Heat the oven beforehand to 325°F (165°C). Grease your baking sheet with thin layer of cooking spray before placing the squash that was cut into half, cut side down.
- Put the squash in the preheated oven and let it bake for 35 minutes or test it by inserting a knife. It's done if a knife can be inserted easily. Remove when done and let it cool.
- While waiting, grease the non-stick saucepan with a cooking spray and heat it over medium heat. Cook the garlic and onion until it reaches golden brown. Mix in the basil, black pepper, tomatoes and bouillon cube and cook for 15 minutes until the sauce is already moderately thick.
- Use a fork to remove the squash strands and keep its shells for later. Spread spoonful of sauce in each half and layer strands of spaghetti squash, some olives, and mozzarella cheese. Repeat same steps to form layers until the shells are all full and until you've used up all the ingredients. Sprinkle Parmesan cheese on top.

- Place it in the preheated oven for 20 minutes until the cheese on top has melted.

Nutrition Information

- Calories: 280 calories;
- Total Carbohydrate: 24.5 g
- Cholesterol: 27 mg
- Total Fat: 15.9 g
- Protein: 14.1 g
- Sodium: 1294 mg

14. Barilla® Super Green Pasta

"This dish has three of our favorite green ingredients."
Serving: 8 | Prep: 10m | Ready in: 25m

Ingredients

- 1 (6.3 oz.) jar Barilla® Traditional Basil Pesto
- 1 (16 oz.) package Barilla® Farfalle
- 1 ripe avocado, halved, pitted and peeled
- 5 cups assorted baby greens such as baby kale, arugula, or spinach
- Fresh basil leaves, torn (optional)
- Shaved Parmesan cheese (optional)

Direction

- Put the avocado and Traditional Basil Pesto in the bowl of a food processor; mix to incorporate; reserve.
- Bring 4 to 6 quarts of water to a rolling boil in a big pot; put in salt to taste and add the Farfalle; mix slowly.
- Cook pasta following packaging instruction; take off heat and drain thoroughly, set aside half cup pasta cooking water.
- Put pasta back to pot; mix in the Traditional Basil Pesto mixture and baby greens; put in pasta water as necessary to reach preferred consistency.
- If wished, top with Parmesan and fresh basil leaves to serve.

Nutrition Information

- Calories: 252 calories;
- Total Carbohydrate: 45.1 g
- Cholesterol: 1 mg
- Total Fat: 4 g
- Protein: 8.3 g
- Sodium: 119 mg

15. Beef And Bow Ties Pasta

"This bow tie pasta recipe combines the classic flavors of ground beef, tomatoes, Italian seasoning, and garlic all in one dish."
Serving: 4 | Prep: 20m | Ready in: 55m

Ingredients

- 1 1/2 cups bow-tie pasta (farfalle)
- 1 lb. ground beef
- 3 cloves garlic, minced
- 2 cups chopped fresh tomatoes
- 3/4 tsp. salt
- 1/4 tsp. black pepper
- 2 tbsps. chopped fresh basil
- 3 tbsps. grated Parmesan cheese

Direction

- Fill a large pot with slightly salted water and set over high heat to a rolling boil. Stir in bow tie pasta at a boil then bring back to a boil. Cook the pasta, uncovered, stirring once in a while, for 12 minutes, until al dente. Using a colander placed in the sink, drain the pasta thoroughly.
- Cook ground beef in a large skillet set on medium heat for 10 minutes until meat is browned and crumbled, then drain off excess fat. Stir in the garlic and cook while stirring often for 5 minutes. Stir in pepper, salt, and tomatoes, and cook, occasionally stirring, for 5 minutes until tomatoes are tender.
- In a big serving dish, place the bow tie pasta and pour the ground beef sauce on top, sprinkle with chopped basil. Gently toss until

combined and serve with a sprinkle of Parmesan cheese.

Nutrition Information

- Calories: 287 calories;
- Total Carbohydrate: 14.7 g
- Cholesterol: 72 mg
- Total Fat: 14.9 g
- Protein: 23.3 g
- Sodium: 564 mg

16. Beef Kebabs With Pomegranate Couscous

"Baharat is a multi-purpose seasoning from the Middle East that is featured in this beef kebab recipe. Bring Middle Eastern flavors to your dinner table with these beef kebabs, some pomegranate couscous and a mouthwatering feta sauce."

Serving: 8 | Prep: 20m | Ready in: 40m

Ingredients

- Feta Sauce:
- 2 oz. feta cheese, crumbled
- 1/4 cup whole-milk plain Greek yogurt
- 1 tsp. lemon juice
- 1/2 tsp. lemon zest
- 1 tbsp. water, or more as needed
- Couscous:
- 2 cups reduced-sodium chicken broth
- 1 1/2 cups Israeli (large pearl) couscous
- 1/3 cup pomegranate seeds
- 1/4 cup chopped pistachios
- 1 tbsp. chopped fresh mint
- 1 tsp. baharat (Middle Eastern spice mix)
- Kebabs:
- 12 oz. beef top sirloin, cut into 1-inch cubes
- 1 tbsp. baharat (Middle Eastern spice mix)
- 1 red bell pepper, cut into 1-inch pieces
- 1 cup cherry tomatoes
- 1 small red onion, cut into 1/2-inch wedges
- 2 portobello mushrooms, stem and ribs removed, cut into 1-inch pieces

Direction

- Make the feta sauce. In a small bowl, mix together feta, lemon juice and zest, and yogurt. Add water in small amounts, with stirring, until preferred consistency is achieved.
- In a medium saucepan, boil the broth and add the couscous. Reduce heat, put the lid on, and simmer until the broth is absorbed and the couscous is cooked through, about 8 to 10 minutes. Use a fork to fluff the cooked couscous. Toss couscous with pistachios, pomegranate seeds, Baharat, and mint.
- Set an outdoor grill to medium, or about 325 to 375 degrees F (160 to 190 degrees C) to pre-heat. Toss the steak cubes with Baharat to coat. Alternately thread steak cubes, tomatoes, mushrooms, onions, and bell peppers onto eight pieces of 10-inch metal skewers. You may also use bamboo skewers that have been left soaking in water for at least half hour.
- Grill for 8 to 12 minutes or until vegetables are cooked and meat is done to liking, turning once or twice during the grill time. Serve with couscous and feta sauce.

Nutrition Information

- Calories: 236 calories;
- Total Carbohydrate: 28.4 g
- Cholesterol: 27 mg
- Total Fat: 6.9 g
- Protein: 15.2 g
- Sodium: 151 mg

17. Bow Tie Medley

"A perfect recipe for a vegetarian pasta dish."
Serving: 12 | Prep: 25m | Ready in: 45m

Ingredients

- 1 (16 oz.) package farfalle (bow tie) pasta
- 1 tbsp. olive oil
- 1/2 red onion, chopped
- 4 cloves garlic, minced

- 1 zucchini, chopped
- 1 yellow squash, chopped
- 1/2 cup sliced fresh mushrooms
- 1/2 red bell pepper, cut into strips
- 5 roma (plum) tomatoes, chopped
- 1/4 cup fresh basil leaves
- 1 tsp. dried oregano
- 1 tsp. salt
- 1 tsp. pepper
- 1/4 cup olive oil
- 1 cup finely grated Parmesan cheese

Direction

- Boil a big pot of lightly salted water. Put in pasta and let cook till al dente for 8 to 10 minutes; drain.
- In a big skillet over medium heat, heat 1 tbsp. olive oil. Sauté 1/2 the chopped tomatoes, bell pepper, mushrooms, yellow squash, zucchini, garlic and onion till soft. Season with pepper, salt, oregano and basil. Put in quarter cup olive oil and pasta. Mix thoroughly, and heat through. Scatter Parmesan and leftover chopped tomatoes on top.

Nutrition Information

- Calories: 243 calories;
- Total Carbohydrate: 32.7 g
- Cholesterol: 6 mg
- Total Fat: 8.6 g
- Protein: 8.9 g
- Sodium: 301 mg

18. Bow Ties With Veggies

"This simple yet tasty recipe tosses farfalle or bow tie pasta with sautéed vegetables."
Serving: 4 | Prep: 15m | Ready in: 25m

Ingredients

- 1 (8 oz.) package farfalle (bow tie) pasta
- 1 tbsp. olive oil
- 1 zucchini, chopped

- 1 large onion, chopped
- salt and pepper to taste

Direction

- Boil water with some salt in a large pot. Add the pasta and cook until al dente, about 8-10 minutes, then drain.
- Over a medium heat, sauté the onion and zucchini with olive oil in skillet until soft. Toss the bow tie pasta along with the vegetables, season with pepper and salt to serve.

Nutrition Information

- Calories: 254 calories;
- Total Carbohydrate: 46.3 g
- Cholesterol: 0 mg
- Total Fat: 4.8 g
- Protein: 8.3 g
- Sodium: 210 mg

19. Bow-tie Pasta With Red Pepper Sauce

"Very simple, yet so tasty."
Serving: 6

Ingredients

- 2 cups red bell pepper, chopped
- 1/2 cup chicken broth
- 1 tbsp. chopped fresh oregano
- 1/4 tsp. salt
- 1/4 tsp. ground black pepper
- 1 tbsp. tomato paste
- 1 tbsp. balsamic vinegar
- 1 tsp. honey
- 2 cups bow tie pasta
- 1 cup blanched green peas
- 2 tbsps. chopped fresh parsley

Direction

- In 2-quart saucepan, put together pepper, salt, oregano, broth and bell pepper. Put cover.

Cook for 20 minutes over medium low heat till bell pepper is soft, mixing from time to time.

- Mix in honey, vinegar and tomato paste; take off heat. In a food processor or blender, puree mixture.
- Meanwhile, cook pasta following packaging instruction. Let drain.
- Put together parsley, peas, red pepper sauce and pasta.

Nutrition Information

- Calories: 95 calories;
- Total Carbohydrate: 18.5 g
- Cholesterol: 0 mg
- Total Fat: 0.7 g
- Protein: 4.2 g
- Sodium: 187 mg

20. Brussels Sprouts 'n Gnocchi

""A simple and nutritious dish filled with onion, gnocchi and Brussels sprouts!""
Serving: 4 | Prep: 15m | Ready in: 32m

Ingredients

- 1 tbsp. olive oil, or more to taste
- 1 lb. fresh Brussels sprouts, thinly sliced
- 1/4 small onion, finely chopped
- 1 clove garlic, minced
- 1 pinch salt and ground black pepper to taste
- 1/4 cup water, or more as needed
- 1 (16 oz.) package frozen gnocchi
- 1 squeeze lemon juice (optional)
- 1 pinch red pepper flakes (optional)

Direction

- Pour olive oil into the big skillet then warm it up at medium heat. Insert the onion and Brussels sprouts, cooking and stirring for around 5 minutes until the onion becomes transparent. Add pepper, salt and garlic, stirring. Add gnocchi and water, leave it simmering with a cover on for around 10 minutes until gnocchi tenderizes and the

water becomes absorbed. Adjust the heat to medium high. Continue cooking and stirring for 2 to 3 minutes until the gnocchi starts browning. Add red pepper flakes and lemon juice, stirring.

Nutrition Information

- Calories: 196 calories;
- Total Carbohydrate: 20.9 g
- Cholesterol: 21 mg
- Total Fat: 11.4 g
- Protein: 3 g
- Sodium: 125 mg

21. Bubble 'n' Squeak II

"Super simple!"
Serving: 8 | Prep: 10m | Ready in: 40m

Ingredients

- 1 (16 oz.) package farfalle (bow tie) pasta
- 1 medium head cabbage, quartered
- 2 tbsps. olive oil
- ground black pepper to taste

Direction

- Boil the lightly salted water in a large pot. Put in farfalle pasta. Cook until al dente or 8-10 mins, then drain.
- In a large skillet, sauté the cabbage in the olive oil over medium heat. Put in a bit more of oil if the pan gets dry. Sauté for about 10 mins. Put in the cooked farfalle pasta. Lower the heat to low, cook for about 20 more mins, stirring occasionally. Sprinkle to taste with pepper.

Nutrition Information

- Calories: 254 calories;
- Total Carbohydrate: 46.4 g
- Cholesterol: 0 mg
- Total Fat: 4.7 g
- Protein: 8.7 g
- Sodium: 11 mg

22. Buttered Noodles

"Simple and delicious."
Serving: 8 | Prep: 5m | Ready in: 15m

Ingredients

- 1 (16 oz.) package fettuccine noodles
- 6 tbsps. butter
- 1/3 cup grated Parmesan cheese
- salt and ground black pepper to taste

Direction

- Put big pot of lightly salted water on rolling boil. Mix fettuccine in; boil. Cook pasta on medium heat for 8-10 minutes till tender yet firm to chew. Drain; put pasta in pot.
- Mix pepper, salt, parmesan cheese and butter into pasta till combined evenly.

Nutrition Information

- Calories: 294 calories;
- Total Carbohydrate: 41.4 g
- Cholesterol: 26 mg
- Total Fat: 10.9 g
- Protein: 8.9 g
- Sodium: 135 mg

23. Butternut Squash Ravioli With Sage-brown Butter Sauce

"This is an easy recipe with complex flavors."
Serving: 8 | Prep: 20m | Ready in: 1h20m

Ingredients

- 1 large butternut squash - halved lengthwise, peeled and seeded
- 2 tsps. butter
- salt and ground black pepper to taste
- 1/2 tsp. allspice
- 1/2 tsp. ground nutmeg
- 2 tsps. ground cinnamon
- 1/2 cup Parmesan cheese
- 50 wonton wrappers
- 1 tsp. egg white, lightly beaten
- Sauce
- 1/4 cup unsalted butter
- 1/4 cup chopped fresh sage leaves
- salt and freshly ground black pepper to taste

Direction

- Preheat the oven to 175°C or 350°F.
- On a baking sheet, put the squash cut side up. In the hollow of each half, put a tbsp. butter. Dust with pepper and salt to taste. With a sheet of aluminum foil tucking in the edges, cover the squash.
- In prepped oven, bake squash for 45 to 65 minutes till tender and easily pricked with a fork.
- Into a bowl, scoop the cooked squash, and crush till smooth. Stir in the Parmesan cheese, cinnamon, nutmeg and allspice till well incorporated. Season with salt and pepper to taste.
- With lightly salted water, fill a deep pot and boil.
- For ravioli, on a clean, flat surface, put a wonton wrapper. With the egg white, brush wrapper edges. Put 1 tbsp. of the squash mixture in the center of the wonton. Put second wonton wrapper over to cover. Redo with the rest of wonton wrappers and squash mixture till all have been used.
- Into the boiling water, drop the ravioli, and allow to cook for 3 to 5 minutes till tender. Take off, drain, and retain warmth till sauce is prepared.
- For the sauce, in a skillet, melt the butter over medium heat. Mix in the sage. Keep cooking and mixing till the sage is crispy yet not browned. Put in pepper and salt to taste. On serving plates, put 6 to 8 raviolis and sprinkle with sauce.

Nutrition Information

- Calories: 271 calories;
- Total Carbohydrate: 40.2 g

- Cholesterol: 27 mg
- Total Fat: 9.2 g
- Protein: 7.9 g
- Sodium: 415 mg

24. Cajun Pasta Fresca

"If you are a fan of pasta, this recipe is totally for you!"
Serving: 8 | Prep: 5m | Ready in: 25m

Ingredients

- 1 lb. vermicelli pasta
- 2 tbsps. olive oil
- 1 tsp. minced garlic
- 13 roma (plum) tomatoes, chopped
- 1 tbsp. salt
- 1 tbsp. chopped fresh parsley
- 1 tbsp. Cajun seasoning
- 1/2 cup shredded mozzarella cheese
- 1/2 cup grated Parmesan cheese

Direction

- Boil the lightly salted water in a large pot. Put in pasta. Cook until al dente or 8-10 mins. Drain.
- In large pan, sauté garlic briefly in oil over medium heat while pasta water is boiling. Stir in the tomatoes and the juice. Season with salt. Use a fork to mash slightly once the tomatoes are bubbly. Mix in the parsley, lower the heat; simmer for 5 more mins.
- Toss the hot pasta with the Parmesan, mozzarella, Cajun seasoning and tomato sauce.

Nutrition Information

- Calories: 294 calories;
- Total Carbohydrate: 46.2 g
- Cholesterol: 9 mg
- Total Fat: 7.5 g
- Protein: 12.2 g
- Sodium: 1178 mg

25. California Primavera

"So easy and so good!!"
Serving: 4

Ingredients

- 6 oz. spaghetti
- 3 tbsps. olive oil
- 1 small onion, chopped
- 2 cloves garlic, minced
- 1 tbsp. chopped fresh basil
- 5 fresh mushrooms, sliced
- 1 (14.5 oz.) can stewed tomatoes
- 1 (16 oz.) package frozen mixed vegetables
- 1 tsp. salt
- ground black pepper to taste
- 1 tbsp. grated Parmesan cheese

Direction

- In large pot, cook spaghetti pasta in the boiling salted water until al dente, then drain.
- In the meantime, heat the olive oil in a large skillet over medium heat. Put in chopped tomatoes, sliced mushrooms, basil, garlic and onion. Cook for 5 mins. Mix in ground black pepper, salt and California-style vegetables. Cook until vegetables are crisp and tender, stirring often, about 10 mins.
- Pour the vegetable mixture over the cooked and drained pasta. Toss well. Top with a sprinkle of grated Parmesan cheese. Enjoy.

Nutrition Information

- Calories: 296 calories;
- Total Carbohydrate: 41.5 g
- Cholesterol: 1 mg
- Total Fat: 11.5 g
- Protein: 8.1 g
- Sodium: 833 mg

26. Cauliflower Fettuccine Alfredo

"You can add garlic, red pepper and a little cream to improve taste."
Serving: 6 | Prep: 15m | Ready in: 1h25m

Ingredients

- 1/2 head cauliflower, cored and cut into small florets
- 2 tbsps. olive oil
- 2 shallots, minced
- 1/2 cup chicken stock
- salt and ground black pepper to taste
- 1/2 lb. fettuccine
- 1 cup grated Parmesan cheese

Direction

- Put steamer insert in saucepan; fill with water to right below bottom of steamer. Boil. Add cauliflower to steamer and cover, then steam for 20 minutes till tender. Cool cauliflower for 15 minutes till cool enough to handle.
- Heat olive oil in skillet on medium heat. Mix and cook shallot for 10 minutes till translucent. Put chicken stock on shallot; cook, for 3 minutes, till heated through. Take off heat. Allow to chill for 15 minutes.
- Mix the cauliflower into shallot mixture. Use a hand blender to whisk till sauce is silky and smooth. Add pepper and salt to season the sauce.
- Put big pot of lightly salted water on rolling boil. Mix fettuccine in; boil again. Cook pasta for 8 minutes on medium heat till cooked through yet firm to bite. Drain.
- Toss sauce and pasta till evenly coated in bowl; sprinkle Parmesan cheese on pasta.

Nutrition Information

- Calories: 258 calories;
- Total Carbohydrate: 33.5 g
- Cholesterol: 12 mg
- Total Fat: 9.3 g
- Protein: 11.8 g
- Sodium: 232 mg

27. Chap Chee Noodles

"Noodle dish you have to try!"
Serving: 4 | Prep: 35m | Ready in: 55m

Ingredients

- 1 tbsp. soy sauce
- 1 tbsp. sesame oil
- 2 green onions, finely chopped
- 1 clove garlic, minced
- 1 tsp. sesame seeds
- 1 tsp. sugar
- 1/4 tsp. black pepper
- 1/3 lb. beef top sirloin, thinly sliced
- 2 tbsps. vegetable oil
- 1/2 cup thinly sliced carrots
- 1/2 cup sliced bamboo shoots, drained
- 1/4 lb. napa cabbage, sliced
- 2 cups chopped fresh spinach
- 3 oz. cellophane noodles, soaked in warm water
- 2 tbsps. soy sauce
- 1 tbsp. sugar
- 1/2 tsp. salt
- 1/4 tsp. black pepper

Direction

- Mix 1/4 tsp. pepper, 1 tsp. sugar, sesame seeds, garlic, green onion, sesame oil and 1 tbsp. soy sauce in a big bowl. Mix in sliced beef. Marinate for 15 minutes in room temperature.
- Heat a big skillet or wok on medium-high heat. Drizzle on oil. Cook beef until it browns evenly. Mix in spinach, napa cabbage, bamboo shoots, and carrots. Add 1/4 tsp. pepper, 1/2 tsp. salt, 1 tbsp. sugar, 2 tbsps. soy sauce, and cellophane noodles. Bring heat to medium and cook until it is heated through.

Nutrition Information

- Calories: 264 calories;
- Total Carbohydrate: 27.9 g

- Cholesterol: 23 mg
- Total Fat: 12.5 g
- Protein: 10.6 g
- Sodium: 1025 mg

28. Chard Stalks And Garlic Scape Pasta

"It's just so delicious!"
Serving: 4 | Prep: 10m | Ready in: 35m

Ingredients

- 1 cup Swiss chard stalks, cut into 1 1/2-inch pieces
- 1 (5 oz.) package dry vermicelli pasta
- 1 tbsp. butter
- 1 tbsp. olive oil
- 1/4 large onion, chopped
- 2 garlic scapes, sliced
- salt and pepper to taste

Direction

- Bring the lightly salted water in large pot to a rolling boil. In the boiling water, cook Swiss chard stems for 10-15 mins until tender; drain, then rinse under cold water. Put aside.
- Bring the lightly salted water in a separate large pot to a rolling boil. In the boiling water, cook vermicelli pasta for 4-5 mins until tender but firm to bite, then drain.
- In the meantime, in a large skillet, melt olive oil with butter over medium heat. Mix in the garlic scapes and onion. Cook while stirring for about 5 mins until onion is translucent and soft. Turn up the heat to medium-high, mix in chard stalks; cook about 5 more mins until onion has browned. Season with pepper and salt; mix in cooked pasta. Enjoy.

Nutrition Information

- Calories: 199 calories;
- Total Carbohydrate: 29.5 g
- Cholesterol: 8 mg

29. Cheese Ravioli With Three Pepper Topping

"A change from tomato sauces."
Serving: 6 | Prep: 15m | Ready in: 35m

Ingredients

- 1 lb. cheese ravioli
- 3 tbsps. olive oil
- 1 small onion, diced
- 1 green bell pepper, thinly sliced
- 1/2 red bell pepper, thinly sliced
- 1/2 yellow bell pepper, thinly sliced
- 2 cups chicken broth, divided
- 1/4 tsp. crushed red pepper flakes

Direction

- Boil a big pot of lightly salted water. In boiling water, cook ravioli for 8 to 10 minutes till done; drain.
- In big skillet, heat olive oil over medium heat. Sauté bell peppers and onion till soft. Put in a cup of the broth, put pepper flakes to season, and let simmer for 5 minutes. Mix in leftover broth, and cook till most of the broth has evaporated. Over ravioli, spoon pepper mixture.

Nutrition Information

- Calories: 255 calories;
- Total Carbohydrate: 27.7 g
- Cholesterol: 30 mg
- Total Fat: 12.4 g
- Protein: 9.1 g
- Sodium: 128 mg

Total Fat: 7.1 g
Protein: 5.5 g
Sodium: 43 mg

30. Cheeseburger Macaroni From Red Gold®

" "They will surely love this cheesy-beef dish even the picky eaters. So fast and healthy; there's no better than this one! Great after a long day, and only takes 25 minutes and you have a meal for dinner." "

Serving: 8 | Prep: 10m | Ready in: 25m

Ingredients

- 1 lb. ground beef
- 1 cup onion, chopped
- 1 (14.5 oz.) can RED GOLD® Petite Diced Tomatoes with Onion, Celery & Green Pepper
- 1 cup water
- 1 cup elbow macaroni
- 2 cups American processed cheese singles, shredded

Direction

- Sear ground beef and onion in a large skillet. Strain well. Put in the water and tomatoes; make it boil.
- Stir in macaroni and make it boil again. Lower heat to gently boil and cook for 10 minutes or until macaroni is done. Dust cheese on top and mix until cheese is dissolved.

Nutrition Information

- Calories: 282 calories;
- Total Carbohydrate: 15.9 g
- Cholesterol: 62 mg
- Total Fat: 15.9 g
- Protein: 18.2 g
- Sodium: 560 mg

31. Cheesy Cauliflower Couscous

" "This recipe can be made so quickly. If you have any couscous leftovers and shredded cheese, try making this one!" "

Serving: 6 | Prep: 15m | Ready in: 30m

Ingredients

- 2 cups cauliflower florets
- 1 cup shredded Cheddar cheese
- 1 1/2 cups cooked couscous
- 1/4 tsp. ground nutmeg
- butter to taste (optional)

Direction

- Set the oven to 375°F or 190°C for preheating. Grease the 8x8-inches baking dish.
- In a microwavable dish, place the cauliflower and microwave it on high setting for 3-4 minutes until tender. Spread the cooked cauliflower into the prepared baking dish. Sprinkle the cauliflower with couscous and Cheddar cheese. Sprinkle nutmeg on the top.
- Let the mixture bake inside the preheated oven for 12-15 minutes until the casserole's top is golden brown and the cheese is melted. Mix in butter according to taste.

Nutrition Information

- Calories: 146 calories;
- Total Carbohydrate: 11.2 g
- Cholesterol: 25 mg
- Total Fat: 8.3 g
- Protein: 6.9 g
- Sodium: 143 mg

32. Cheesy Ramen Noodles

"A great way to make ramen noodles. Great for college students!"
Serving: 1 | Ready in: 5m

Ingredients

- 2 cups water
- 1 (3 oz.) package any flavor ramen noodles
- 1 slice American cheese

Direction

- Boil water in a saucepan. Put ramen noodles. Cook till tender for 2 minutes. Pour water out. Mix cheese and seasoning packet in. Serve.

Nutrition Information

- Calories: 163 calories;
- Total Carbohydrate: 7.9 g
- Cholesterol: 27 mg
- Total Fat: 11.3 g
- Protein: 7.5 g
- Sodium: 733 mg

33. Chick'n Parmesan Casserole

"Super tasty!"
Serving: 8 | Prep: 10m | Ready in: 45m

Ingredients

- 2 (15 oz.) cans tomato sauce
- 1 tsp. dried basil
- 1 tsp. extra-virgin olive oil
- 1/4 cup grated Parmesan cheese
- 1 clove garlic, minced
- 1 dash white pepper
- 1/2 (16 oz.) package uncooked rotini pasta
- 1/2 (12 oz.) package artificial chicken tenders (such as Quorn™ Chik'n Tenders), cut in half
- 1/2 cup shredded mozzarella cheese

Direction

- Start preheating oven to 325°F (165°C).
- In a saucepan, simmer white pepper, garlic, Parmesan cheese, olive oil, basil and tomato sauce over medium-high heat. Lower the heat to low, keep at a simmer. Bring the lightly salted water in a large pot to a rolling boil over high heat. Stir in rotini when water is boiling. Bring back to a boil. Cook, uncovered, for about 8 mins until pasta is cooked through yet still firm to the bite, stirring occasionally. Stir in artificial chicken once rotini is nearly ready. Drain well.
- Spread bottom of the 2-qt casserole dish with 1/2 pasta sauce. Put in drained pasta mixture. Pour remaining sauce on top of pasta. Sprinkle mozzarella cheese over. Bake in preheated oven for about 20 mins until cheese is browned lightly and bubbly.

Nutrition Information

- Calories: 188 calories;
- Total Carbohydrate: 29.4 g
- Cholesterol: 7 mg
- Total Fat: 3.5 g
- Protein: 10.8 g
- Sodium: 722 mg

34. Chicken Bolognaise

"This dish is so hearty."
Serving: 8 | Prep: 15m | Ready in: 40m

Ingredients

- 1 tbsp. vegetable oil
- 3 skinless, boneless chicken breast halves - cut into 1 inch cubes
- 1 white onion, chopped
- 2 cloves garlic, finely chopped
- 1 (28 oz.) can peeled and crushed tomatoes
- 4 button mushrooms, chopped
- 1/2 tsp. white sugar
- 1/2 tsp. Italian seasoning
- 4 cups uncooked rotini pasta
- 1/4 cup grated Parmesan cheese for topping

Direction

- In a large skillet, heat oil over medium heat. Put in garlic, onion and chicken; sauté for about 10 mins until the chicken has mostly cooked through. Mix in Italian seasoning, mushrooms and crushed tomatoes. Cook, stirring frequently, for about 5 mins.
- Lower the heat; stir in sugar. Simmer at least 15 mins. In the meantime, boil the lightly salted water in a large pot; put in the rotini pasta. Cook until al dente, then drain. Top with chicken mixture and grated Parmesan cheese to serve.

Nutrition Information

- Calories: 288 calories;
- Total Carbohydrate: 46.3 g
- Cholesterol: 27 mg
- Total Fat: 4.6 g
- Protein: 19.7 g
- Sodium: 195 mg

35. Chicken Pasta I

"It is low in calories and fat but delicious."
Serving: 8 | Prep: 30m | Ready in: 45m

Ingredients

- 3 cups mostaccioli
- 3 skinless, boneless chicken breast halves
- 1/4 onion, chopped
- 3 fresh mushrooms, sliced
- 2 tbsps. Italian seasoning
- 1 (14.5 oz.) can diced tomatoes
- salt and pepper to taste
- 2 tbsps. grated Parmesan cheese

Direction

- Boil the lightly salted water in a large pot. Put in pasta. Cook until al dente or 8-10 mins; drain, then reserve.
- In the meantime, in the large lightly greased skillet, cook chicken over medium heat for

about 15 mins. Take away from the pan. Let cool, then dice.
- In a large skillet, combine pepper, salt, tomatoes with juice, Italian seasoning, mushrooms and onion over medium heat; cook until the onions are translucent. Take away from the heat. Put in pasta and chicken. Add a sprinkle of Parmesan cheese on top. Enjoy.

Nutrition Information

- Calories: 185 calories;
- Total Carbohydrate: 26.1 g
- Cholesterol: 27 mg
- Total Fat: 1.8 g
- Protein: 15.7 g
- Sodium: 165 mg

36. Chicken Ro*tel® Spaghetti

"This dish never fails to get compliments."
Serving: 20 | Prep: 15m | Ready in: 1h25m

Ingredients

- cooking spray
- 4 large skinless, boneless chicken breast halves
- 1 (12 oz.) package spaghetti
- 3/4 cup butter
- 2 large onions, chopped
- 2 green bell peppers, chopped
- 2 (10 oz.) cans diced tomatoes with green chile peppers (such as RO*TEL®)
- 1 (16 oz.) package process cheese food (such as Velveeta®), cut into small cubes
- 1 (16 oz.) package frozen peas
- 1 (16 oz.) can mushrooms, drained
- 1/2 cup sliced olives
- 1/2 cup chopped black olives

Direction

- Start preheating the oven to 350°F (175°C). Prepare 2 baking dishes (9x13-inch) with cooking spray.

- Boil water in a pot. In boiling water, cook chicken for 7-10 mins until the juices run clear and chicken is no longer pink in middle. An instant-read thermometer should register at least 165°F (74°C) when inserted into the middle. Transfer chicken on the cutting board to cool, leaving at least six cups of the water in pot.
- In the boiling water, cook the spaghetti for about 12 minutes until cooked through yet firm to bite, stirring occasionally, then drain.
- In a large pot, melt butter over medium heat. In hot butter, cook while stirring bell peppers and onion for 5-7 mins until softened. Put in cheese food cubes. Cook until cheese melts and becomes smooth, stirring occasionally. Cut the chicken into small pieces. Mix into cheese mixture. Stir chopped olives, sliced olives, mushrooms, peas and drained spaghetti into cheese sauce; distribute between the prepared baking dishes.
- Bake in the preheated oven for about 45 minutes until bubbly.

Nutrition Information

- Calories: 298 calories;
- Total Carbohydrate: 20.7 g
- Cholesterol: 63 mg
- Total Fat: 16.1 g
- Protein: 18.2 g
- Sodium: 698 mg

---

37. Chicken Taco Lasagna

"It is the best chicken taco ever!"
Serving: 8 | Prep: 20m | Ready in: 1h35m

Ingredients

- 4 boneless skinless chicken breasts, cut into 1/4-inch strips
- ½ cup lime juice
- 2 (1 oz.) packets taco seasoning mix
- 1 ½ cups shredded mozzarella cheese, divided

- 1 cup sour cream
- 1 cup salsa
- salt and ground black pepper to taste
- 1 (8 oz.) package no-boil lasagna noodles, or to taste

Direction

- In large bowl, combine taco seasoning, lime juice and chicken. Stir to ensure that the chicken is covered evenly.
- Cook the chicken mixture for about 15 mins over medium heat, until it is firm.
- In a bowl, mix salsa, sour cream and half cup of mozzarella cheese. Season with pepper and salt.
- In the bottom of a baking dish (9x9 inches), put a few spoonfuls sour cream mixture. Layer on top the noodles and the chicken. Add the remaining one cup of mozzarella cheese to cover
- Bake in preheated oven for about 60 mins until the cheese melts and noodles become tender.

Nutrition Information

- Calories: 271 calories;
- Total Carbohydrate: 21.6 g
- Cholesterol: 57 mg
- Total Fat: 11.4 g
- Protein: 19.9 g
- Sodium: 905 mg

---

38. Chicken Veggie Stir Fry

"A well-loved recipe by my family."
Serving: 8 | Prep: 15m | Ready in: 30m

Ingredients

- 3 tbsps. vegetable oil
- 3 skinless, boneless chicken breast halves - cut into strips
- 2 stalks celery, chopped
- 2 zucchini, quartered and sliced
- 10 mushrooms, sliced

- 2 cups chopped spinach
- 1 (3 oz.) package ramen noodle pasta with flavor packet
- 1 cup uncooked long-grain rice
- 1 tbsp. cornstarch
- 1/4 cup cold water
- 1 tsp. vegetable oil
- 1/4 cup soy sauce

Direction

- In a wok/big skillet, heat oil. Sauté chicken till cooked through and not pink in color.
- Mix zucchini and celery in. Stir-fry for 3 minutes. Add spinach and mushrooms. Stir fry for 2 more minutes. Lower heat to low; simmer.
- Meanwhile in a medium saucepan, boil salted water. Add rice. Lower heat. Cover. Simmer it for 20 minutes. Follow package directions to prepare ramen noodles. Mix ramen into prepared rice; put aside.
- Mix soy sauce, oil, water and cornstarch well in a small bowl. Mix into veggies and chicken then into noodles and rice. Mix everything together. Simmer for 5 more minutes. Serve while hot.

Nutrition Information

- Calories: 263 calories;
- Total Carbohydrate: 31 g
- Cholesterol: 27 mg
- Total Fat: 9 g
- Protein: 14.3 g
- Sodium: 695 mg

39. Chipotle Chicken Skillet

"This recipe will surprise you."
Serving: 6 | Prep: 10m | Ready in: 50m

Ingredients

- 2 prepared chicken breasts, cut into 1-inch cubes, purchase prepared or cook your own

- 1 (14.5 oz.) can RED GOLD® Petite Diced Tomatoes with Chipotle
- 1 cup water
- 1 (6 oz.) package egg noodles

Direction

- Combine water, chicken and diced tomatoes in electric skillet. Heat to boiling; lower the heat to simmer; cook for 20 mins.
- Mix in egg noodles. Cook until mixture has thickened, and noodles are tender or 20 more mins. Enjoy immediately. Option: Enjoy over mashed potatoes or rice.

Nutrition Information

- Calories: 170 calories;
- Total Carbohydrate: 24.8 g
- Cholesterol: 43 mg
- Total Fat: 2 g
- Protein: 11.9 g
- Sodium: 244 mg

40. Cilantro And Parsley Shrimp

"This sauce is great over pasta."
Serving: 4 | Prep: 15m | Ready in: 25m

Ingredients

- 4 oz. uncooked angel hair pasta (optional)
- olive oil
- 1 lb. uncooked medium shrimp, peeled and deveined
- 1 onion, chopped
- 10 sun-dried tomatoes, cut into strips
- 4 cloves garlic, minced
- 1/2 bunch chopped fresh parsley
- 1/2 bunch chopped fresh cilantro

Direction

- Put lightly salted water in a big pot and over high heat, bring to a rolling boil. Once boiling, stir angel hair pasta in and continue boiling. Cook the pasta without cover for 4 to 5 minutes until pasta has cooked through, but is still firm to bite, stirring occasionally. With a colander set in the sink, drain it.

- Over medium-high heat, heat the olive oil in a big skillet. Stir in onion and shrimp. Cook and stir for about 2 minutes until the shrimp are starting to turn pink. Stir in garlic and sun-dried tomatoes. Continue cooking for about 4 minutes until the onion has turned translucent and the shrimp are no longer opaque in the center. Stir in cilantro and parsley. To serve, pour it over pasta.

Nutrition Information

- Calories: 241 calories;
- Total Carbohydrate: 25.1 g
- Cholesterol: 173 mg
- Total Fat: 5.4 g
- Protein: 23.4 g
- Sodium: 370 mg

---

41. Couscous With Mushrooms And Sun-dried Tomatoes

"Hearty Portobello mushrooms and lively sun-dried tomatoes are mixed with couscous in this satisfying entree."
Serving: 4 | Prep: 30m | Ready in: 45m

Ingredients

- 1 cup dehydrated sun-dried tomatoes
- 1 1/2 cups water
- 1/2 (10 oz.) package couscous
- 1 tsp. olive oil
- 3 cloves garlic, pressed
- 1 bunch green onions, chopped
- 1/3 cup fresh basil leaves
- 1/4 cup fresh cilantro, chopped
- 1/2 lemon, juiced
- salt and pepper to taste
- 4 oz. portobello mushroom caps, sliced

Direction

- Transfer the sun-dried tomatoes into a bowl containing one cup of water. Let it soak for 30 minutes until rehydrated. Drain the tomatoes, save the water, and then chop them.
- Mix the reserved sun-dried tomato water with enough water to yield 1 1/2 cups in a medium saucepan. Heat to a boil. Mix in couscous. Cover the pan, take out from the heat source and let it stand for 5 minutes until the liquid has been absorbed. Carefully fluff with a fork.
- Heat olive oil in a skillet and then mix in the green onions, sun-dried tomatoes, and garlic. Cook while stirring for about 5 minutes until the green onions become tender. Stir in the lemon juice, basil, and cilantro. Season with pepper and salt. Stir in mushrooms and continue to cook for 3 to 5 minutes. Mix with the cooked couscous and serve.

Nutrition Information

- Calories: 178 calories;
- Total Carbohydrate: 36.1 g
- Cholesterol: 0 mg
- Total Fat: 2 g
- Protein: 7.5 g
- Sodium: 300 mg

---

42. Crab Casserole

"Delicious and creative!"
Serving: 6 | Prep: 20m | Ready in: 1h5m

Ingredients

- 1 (8 oz.) package egg noodles
- 3/4 cup low-fat mayonnaise
- 1 tsp. Worcestershire sauce
- 3 tbsps. ketchup
- 1 chopped onions
- 1 large green bell pepper, chopped
- 1 1/2 cups cooked crabmeat
- 1 (4 oz.) can small shrimp, drained
- 1 cup diced celery

- salt and pepper to taste
- 1/4 cup dry bread crumbs

Direction

- Preheat an oven to 175°C/350°F.
- Cook pasta till al dente in big pot with salted boiling water; drain. Put into big bowl.
- Add onion, ketchup, Worcestershire sauce and mayonnaise in noodles; stir well. Mix celery, shrimp, crab, green pepper, pepper and salt to taste. Put mixture in 8x8-inch casserole dish. Sprinkle bread crumbs on casserole to taste.
- In preheated oven, bake till bubbly and brown for 35 minutes.

Nutrition Information

- Calories: 245 calories;
- Total Carbohydrate: 36 g
- Cholesterol: 89 mg
- Total Fat: 2.8 g
- Protein: 18.4 g
- Sodium: 310 mg

43. Creamy Asparagus Pasta

""This meal is easy to prepare and is amazingly tasty and filling!""
Serving: 8 | Prep: 5m | Ready in: 30m

Ingredients

- 1 lb. fresh asparagus, trimmed and cut into 2 inch pieces
- 2 tbsps. butter
- 1 clove garlic, minced
- 1 pint light cream
- 1 lb. linguine pasta
- 1 lemon, juiced

Direction

- Boil a pot of water then add asparagus and boil for 3 to 4 minutes then drain.
- Melt butter over medium heat in a big cooking pan. Sauté the asparagus and garlic in the butter for 3 to 4 minutes. Pour the cream, stirring it in and let it simmer for 10 minutes.
- Boil another large pot of water then add and cook the linguine in it for 8 to 10 minutes, until the pasta is al dente; drain completely then move the linguine to a serving platter.
- Combine the lemon juice, stirring it into the asparagus mixture then pour this mixture over pasta.

Nutrition Information

- Calories: 247 calories;
- Total Carbohydrate: 44 g
- Cholesterol: 10 mg
- Total Fat: 4.7 g
- Protein: 8.3 g
- Sodium: 31 mg

44. Creamy Chicken Pasta

"It's refreshing, light and very tasty."
Serving: 6

Ingredients

- 8 oz. wide egg noodles
- 1/2 cup frozen green peas
- 3 skinless, boneless chicken breast halves
- 1 (10.75 oz.) can condensed cream of mushroom soup
- 1/3 cup milk
- 1/4 cup mozzarella cheese

Direction

- Cook the egg noodles in medium pot of the boiling salted water. Once the pasta is 3 mins away from being cooked, put in broccoli or frozen peas. Cook until noodles and vegetables are tender, then drain well.
- In the meantime, in a medium saucepan, boil chicken until it is completely cooked. Drain the chicken, then cut into bite size pieces.
- Mix milk and cream of mushroom soup in a large saucepan until lumps dissolve and the mixture is warm.

- Put vegetables, noodles and cooked and chopped chicken into large saucepan. Blend milk and soup mixture with ingredients. Mix in the grated mozzarella cheese until it is melted.
- Enjoy warm.

Nutrition Information

- Calories: 282 calories;
- Total Carbohydrate: 32.5 g
- Cholesterol: 70 mg
- Total Fat: 6.7 g
- Protein: 21.9 g
- Sodium: 423 mg

45. Creamy Chicken With Pasta And Broccoli

"Your kids will very like this!"
Serving: 12 | Prep: 15m | Ready in: 35m

Ingredients

- 1 lb. uncooked spaghetti
- 1 lb. broccoli florets
- 1 tbsp. margarine
- 1 lb. skinless, boneless chicken breast halves - cut into strips
- 1/2 cup chopped onions
- 1 (10.75 oz.) can condensed cream of chicken soup
- 2/3 cup milk
- 2/3 cup water
- 1 (3 oz.) package cream cheese, cubed and softened
- 3/4 cup grated Parmesan cheese

Direction

- Boil the lightly salted water in a large pot. In the pot, put spaghetti. Cook for 4 mins. Mix in broccoli florets. Keep cooking until the spaghetti is al dente or 4-6 mins. Drain, then place into a large bowl.

- In a skillet, melt margarine over medium heat. Cook onion and chicken for 5 mins until the onions become tender and chicken juices run clear.
- Whisk cream cheese, milk, water and soup together in a bowl until they become smooth. Stir with onion and chicken into skillet. Boil. Lower the heat to low, simmer until it is thickened slightly or for 5 mins. In the bowl, toss with broccoli and spaghetti to Enjoy.

Nutrition Information

- Calories: 280 calories;
- Total Carbohydrate: 33 g
- Cholesterol: 38 mg
- Total Fat: 8.5 g
- Protein: 17.7 g
- Sodium: 314 mg

46. Creamy Poblano Mac & Cheese

""With the addition of stir fried fresh vegetables and creamy poblano and queso soup, this mac 'n cheese turns extraordinary. This satisfying casserole is amazingly great, simple to make and guaranteed to earn good feedback!""
Serving: 8 | Prep: 20m | Ready in: 30m

Ingredients

- 1 tbsp. butter
- 1 medium onion, chopped
- 1/2 cup red bell pepper, chopped
- 1 cup medium tomato, chopped
- 1 clove garlic, chopped
- 1/8 tsp. salt
- 1/8 tsp. ground black pepper
- 1 (10.75 oz.) can Campbell's® Condensed Creamy Poblano & Queso Soup
- 3/4 cup milk
- 1 cup shredded Cheddar cheese
- 8 oz. elbow macaroni, cooked and drained
- 2 tbsps. chopped cilantro

Direction

- In a 3-qt.saucepan over medium high heat, put butter to heat. Stir in the pepper and onion and cook for 5 minutes or until the veggies are soft, mixing occasionally.
- Stir garlic and tomato into the saucepan and cook for 1 minute.
- Add black pepper and salt to taste.
- Mix in the milk and soup and let it boil. Separate the saucepan from the heat. Put in the cheese and mix until dissolved. Mix in the macaroni. Top with cilantro.

Nutrition Information

- Calories: 240 calories;
- Total Carbohydrate: 28.6 g
- Cholesterol: 22 mg
- Total Fat: 9.9 g
- Protein: 9.1 g
- Sodium: 420 mg

---

47. Creamy Shrimp Casserole

"A recipe that yields a lot!"
Serving: 8 | Prep: 20m | Ready in: 1h35m

Ingredients

- 1 lb. shrimp, peeled and deveined
- 1 tsp. salt
- 3 cups wide egg noodles
- 2 tbsps. butter
- 1 1/2 tbsps. all-purpose flour
- 2 1/2 cups milk
- 1/2 cup heavy cream
- salt and ground black pepper to taste
- 1 cup frozen green peas, thawed
- 1 (4.5 oz.) can sliced mushrooms, drained (optional)
- 1 cup crushed buttery round crackers
- 1 tbsp. cold butter, thinly sliced

Direction

- Preheat an oven to 175°C/350°F. Grease 3-quart casserole dish lightly.
- Use water to fill big pot; boil on high heat. Mix shrimp in; lower heat to simmer. Cook shrimp for 3 minutes till bright pink and opaque. Transfer shrimp to a bowl using slotted spoon. Put water on full rolling boil on high heat; mix noodles in. Cook for 8 minutes till noodles are tender. In a colander set in sink, drain.
- Melt 2 tbsps. of butter in saucepan on medium heat. Mix flour into butter to create a paste. Take pan off heat. Whisk cream and milk slowly in till smooth. Season with black pepper and salt to taste. Put sauce on heat; reduce heat to simmer. Constantly whisk for 5 minutes till sauce is thick.
- Put noodles in the prepared casserole dish. Top with cooked shrimp, mushrooms and peas. Put sauce on casserole. Evenly sprinkle crushed cracker crumbs on top. Use 6 thin butter slices to dot top of casserole.
- In preheated oven, bake for 1 hour till cracker topping is golden brown and crisp.

Nutrition Information

- Calories: 263 calories;
- Total Carbohydrate: 22.9 g
- Cholesterol: 126 mg
- Total Fat: 11.9 g
- Protein: 15.9 g
- Sodium: 614 mg

---

48. Creamy Tomato-basil Pasta With Shrimp

"A combination of fresh tomatoes and chopped basil along with shrimp and pasta, a seriously high-end entrée."
Serving: 4 | Prep: 15m | Ready in: 25m

Ingredients

- 3 cups farfalle (bow tie) pasta, uncooked

- 1/4 cup KRAFT Sun-Dried Tomato Vinaigrette Dressing, divided
- 1 lb. uncooked medium shrimp, peeled and deveined
- 1 cup fat-free reduced-sodium chicken broth
- 1/2 tsp. garlic powder
- 1/2 tsp. black pepper
- 4 oz. PHILADELPHIA Neufchatel Cheese, 1/3 Less Fat than Cream Cheese
- 2 cups grape tomatoes
- 1/2 cup KRAFT Shredded Parmesan Cheese
- 8 fresh basil leaves, cut into strips

Direction

- Cook pasta following packaging instruction. In the meantime, in big skillet on medium heat, heat 2 tbsps. dressing. Put in shrimp; cook and mix for 2 to 3 minutes till shrimp becomes pink. Take off shrimp from skillet with a slotted spoon; put cover to retain warmth. Throw any drippings in skillet.
- Mix in seasonings, broth and leftover dressing to skillet; allow to cook for 2 minutes till heated through. Put in Neufchatel; cook and mix for 2 to 3 minutes till melted. Mix in tomatoes and cook for a minute.
- Drain the pasta. Combine to ingredients in skillet. Mix in half the basil and Parmesan; atop with shrimp and the rest of the basil.

Nutrition Information

- Calories: 286 calories;
- Total Carbohydrate: 26.7 g
- Cholesterol: 184 mg
- Total Fat: 7.7 g
- Protein: 27.6 g
- Sodium: 633 mg

49. Easy Chicken Skillet

"An easy and quick stir-fry chicken featuring ramen noodles."
Serving: 4 | Prep: 15m | Ready in: 30m

Ingredients

- 1 tbsp. canola oil
- 3 skinless, boneless chicken breast halves - trimmed and cut into large pieces
- 1 1/2 cups water
- 2 (3 oz.) packages chicken-flavored ramen noodles, broken into pieces
- 2 cloves garlic, crushed
- 1 red bell pepper, chopped
- 1 cup frozen broccoli
- 4 green onions, chopped
- 1 tbsp. dried parsley
- 1 tbsp. soy sauce

Direction

- In a big skillet, heat canola oil on medium high heat. Stir and cook chicken for about 5 minutes till juices are clear and chicken isn't pink in the middle. Add 1 ramen seasoning packet, ramen noodles and water; mix to combine,
- Mix soy sauce, parsley, green onions, broccoli, red bell pepper and garlic into chicken-broth mixture; boil. Lower heat. Simmer for about 10 minutes, occasionally mixing, till noodles are cooked through yet firm to chew and broccoli is cooked.

Nutrition Information

- Calories: 298 calories;
- Total Carbohydrate: 33.7 g
- Cholesterol: 49 mg
- Total Fat: 5.3 g
- Protein: 28.3 g
- Sodium: 752 mg

50. Easy Homemade Pad Thai

"This is the recipe with full Asian flavor made from a
number of delicious ingredients."
Serving: 4 | Prep: 5m | Ready in: 10m

Ingredients

- 4 oz. pad Thai rice noodles
- 2 tsps. vegetable oil
- 1 egg
- 1/2 cup water
- 2 tbsps. crunchy peanut butter
- 2 tbsps. soy sauce
- 2 tbsps. lime juice
- 2 tsps. packed brown sugar
- 1/2 tsp. McCormick® Ginger, Ground
- 1/4 tsp. McCormick® Red Pepper, Crushed
- 1 cup bean sprouts

Direction

- Cook noodles according to package directions.
- In a large skillet or a wok over medium-high heat, heat oil. Put in egg; cook for 30 seconds with stirs (the egg won't be completely cooked).
- Add the remaining ingredients and cooked noodles apart from bean sprouts; stir to combine. Let cook for about 1 minute with stirs until the noodles absorb most of the cooking liquid. Add bean sprouts and stir. Add lime wedges, sliced green onions and crushed peanuts to serve to your interest.

Nutrition Information

- Calories: 209 calories;
- Total Carbohydrate: 29.9 g
- Cholesterol: 46 mg
- Total Fat: 7.8 g
- Protein: 5.6 g
- Sodium: 562 mg

51. Easy Mac 'n' Cheese

""I used to prepare this super simple and great tastes recipe
and now my kid enjoys it better than the real thing!""
Serving: 4 | Prep: 2m | Ready in: 15m

Ingredients

- 1 cup macaroni
- 1/2 cup process cheese sauce
- 2 frankfurters, sliced
- 1 tsp. grated Parmesan cheese
- 1 pinch dried oregano
- 4 buttery round crackers, crushed

Direction

- Prepare the oven by preheating to 350°F (175°C). Place lightly salted water in a big pot and make it boil. Put in the pasta and cook for 8-10 minutes or until al dente; strain. Put cheese sauce in a microwave to heat for 1 minute. Mix in an 8x8-inch baking dish the oregano, Parmesan, sliced frankfurters, cheese sauce and cooked pasta. Place crumbled crackers on top and bake in the oven for 10 minutes.

Nutrition Information

- Calories: 284 calories;
- Total Carbohydrate: 25.9 g
- Cholesterol: 36 mg
- Total Fat: 14.9 g
- Protein: 10.8 g
- Sodium: 829 mg

52. Easy One-pot Pasta Puttanesca

"This dish will please everyone."
Serving: 6

Ingredients

- 1 (24 oz.) jar Ragu® Hearty Traditional Sauce
- 2 cups water

- 1 (8 oz.) package uncooked spaghetti
- 1 (14 oz.) can quartered artichoke hearts
- 4 oz. pitted and halved black kalamata olives
- 2 tbsps. capers
- 3 cloves garlic, minced
- 1 cup halved grape tomatoes
- 2 tsps. crushed red pepper
- 2 tbsps. chopped fresh parsley

Direction

- In a large pot, combine water and Ragu(R) Sauce. If desired, break spaghetti in 1/2. Put into pot. Boil, stirring often.
- Mix in parsley, crushed red pepper flakes, grape tomatoes, garlic, capers, kalamata olives and artichoke hearts. Lower the heat to medium-low, simmer, covered, for 8-10 mins, stirring frequently, until the pasta is cooked to the preferred tenderness.
- Take away from the heat. Enjoy warm. If desired, decorate with red pepper and extra fresh parsley.

Nutrition Information

- Calories: 297 calories;
- Total Carbohydrate: 47.3 g
- Cholesterol: 0 mg
- Total Fat: 8.2 g
- Protein: 8.8 g
- Sodium: 1326 mg

53. Easy Red Pasta Sauce

"This basic yet tasty red sauce can be made with canned tomatoes or with fresh ones during the summer months. You can add in more red pepper flakes for a spicy kick."
Serving: 6 | Prep: 25m | Ready in: 1h

Ingredients

- 4 tbsps. olive oil
- 2 cloves garlic
- 1/4 cup chopped onion
- 2 tbsps. dried parsley

- 1 tbsp. dried basil
- ground black pepper to taste
- 1 (29 oz.) can Italian-style stewed tomatoes, drained
- 1 pinch crushed red pepper flakes
- 12 oz. angel hair pasta

Direction

- Heat oil using a medium-sized pan on low heat and sauté and heat through the garlic until it turns translucent and not brown. Add onion and cook over low heat until translucent for 5-10 minutes.
- Stir in the ground black pepper, basil, and parsley, then add the tomatoes and cover the saucepan. Turn up stove up to medium and heat until it to a strong simmer. Reduce the heat then add in red pepper flakes. Cover saucepan and cook for 25-35 minutes.
- You can blend the sauce in a food processor for 2-3 seconds to make it a more uniform sauce, or let it cook, uncovered, on medium-low heat for 10 minutes until thick.
- Boil a large pot filled with lightly salt water. Add in the pasta and cook until al dente, about 6-8 minutes. Drain then serve along with the sauce.

Nutrition Information

- Calories: 284 calories;
- Total Carbohydrate: 41.2 g
- Cholesterol: 0 mg
- Total Fat: 10.6 g
- Protein: 7.4 g
- Sodium: 405 mg

54. Easy Shrimp Lo Mein

" "It's super simple to make this Chinese delicacy. You can use a seasoned wok to make better results with the searing." "

Serving: 2 | Prep: 10m | Ready in: 35m

Ingredients

- 1 (8 oz.) package spaghetti
- 2 tbsps. soy sauce
- 2 tbsps. oyster sauce
- 2 tbsps. brown sugar
- 2 tsps. fish sauce
- 1/2 tsp. garlic powder
- 1/2 tsp. ground ginger
- 2 tsps. vegetable oil
- 1 lb. uncooked medium shrimp, peeled and deveined
- 1 cup chopped broccoli
- 1/4 yellow onion, thinly sliced
- 3 crimini mushrooms, sliced
- 2 cloves garlic, minced
- 2 large eggs

Direction

- Boil a large pot of water with a bit of salt. Let the spaghetti cook for 12 minutes until cooked through yet firm to the bite, and then remove the water.
- In a bowl, combine the oyster sauce, soy sauce, brown sugar, garlic powder, fish sauce, and ground ginger until the sugar is completely dissolved.
- Set the heat to medium and use a large wok or skillet to heat the oil. Let the shrimp cook in the hot oil while stirring for 1 to 2 minutes until its color changes. Mix in the onion, mushrooms, and broccoli then cook for 3 to 5 minutes or until it starts softening. Add the garlic to the vegetable mixture. Position the vegetables onto a side of the pan. Then, cook eggs in the available space and lightly scramble them for 3 to 5 minutes, or until no longer moist. Mix the egg with the vegetables and shrimp. Combine the cooked noodles with the sauce, then stir them all together to cook

for another 2 minutes until hot mixed well. Serve right away.

Nutrition Information

- Calories: 834 calories;
- Total Carbohydrate: 109.5 g
- Cholesterol: 531 mg
- Total Fat: 14.3 g
- Protein: 63.9 g
- Sodium: 2240 mg

55. Easy Sriracha Noodles

"This one is a must-try!"

Serving: 5 | Prep: 10m | Ready in: 20m

Ingredients

- 1 (10 oz.) package egg noodles
- 3 1/2 tbsps. sriracha sauce
- 1 tbsp. butter
- 1 tbsp. peanut oil
- 1 tbsp. rice vinegar
- 1 1/2 tsps. dried basil
- 1 tsp. paprika
- freshly cracked black pepper

Direction

- Boil lightly salted water in a pot. In boiling water, cook the egg noodles for about 5 mins until cooked through yet firm to bite, stirring occasionally. Drain, then put noodles into a bowl.
- In the same pot, stir together black pepper, paprika, basil, rice vinegar, peanut oil, butter and sriracha sauce over medium heat for 3-5 mins until the sauce is heated through and smooth. Put noodles into sauce; coat by tossing. Let cool, then serve.

Nutrition Information

- Calories: 270 calories;
- Total Carbohydrate: 42 g
- Cholesterol: 54 mg

- Total Fat: 7.6 g
- Protein: 8.2 g
- Sodium: 473 mg

56. Easy Tofu Shirataki Stir-fry Style

"This stir-fry-style dish is made with tofu shirataki noodles."
Serving: 2 | Prep: 5m | Ready in: 15m

Ingredients

- 1 (16 oz.) package frozen vegetable medley (such as Green Giant®)
- 1 (8 oz.) package angel hair-style tofu shirataki noodles, or to taste
- 1/2 tsp. minced garlic
- 2 tsps. soy sauce, or more to taste
- 1/2 tsp. ground ginger, or more to taste

Direction

- In the bag, microwave vegetables for about 5 minutes until thawed and heated through. For about a minute, let it cool. Open the pouch.
- Thoroughly rinse and drain the shirataki noodles, then, put it in a microwave-safe bowl. Cook noodles for about a minute until mostly heated through in the microwave. Over medium heat, heat a saucepan. Put garlic and cook for a minute until fragrant. Put ginger, soy sauce, mixed vegetables and cooked noodles. Cook and stir for 2 to 3 minutes until flavors blend and heated through. Put hot sauce.

Nutrition Information

- Calories: 139 calories;
- Total Carbohydrate: 29.8 g
- Cholesterol: 0 mg
- Total Fat: 0 g
- Protein: 5.7 g
- Sodium: 628 mg

57. Eggplant And Ground Beef Lasagna

"A tasty combo of moussaka and lasagna. Spinach flavored lasagna pasta taste great with this. Try ground lamb for a different taste."
Serving: 8 | Prep: 15m | Ready in: 1h20m

Ingredients

- 9 lasagna noodles
- 1/2 lb. ground beef
- 1 onion, chopped
- 4 fresh mushrooms, sliced
- 2 cloves garlic, crushed
- 2 (14.5 oz.) cans Italian-flavored crushed tomatoes
- 1 eggplant, peeled and thinly sliced
- 2 cups mozzarella and cheddar cheese blend

Direction

- Preheat the oven to 175 degrees C (350 degrees F). Grease the sides and bottom of a 9x13in. baking dish.
- Roll boil a large pot of slightly salted water. Cook lasagna pasta for 10 minutes at a boil until tender yet firm to the bite. Strain pasta and set aside.
- Stir onion, mushrooms, garlic and ground beef in a skillet. Use medium heat until beef is completely brown; about 10 minutes.
- Add in canned tomatoes into ground beef; gently boil until sauce has formed about 3 to 4 min.
- Pour about one-fourth of the sauce into the bottom of the prepared baking dish.
- Layer pasta on top of sauce. Place a thin layer of sauce above the pasta. Place a layer of eggplant slices above the sauce layer and top of noodle, drizzle a fourth of cheese on top of the eggplant slices. Repeat the layers with remaining ingredients until ending with a layer of sauce topped with the remaining cheese. Bake in preheated oven until cheese is bubbly and top is brown; about 40 minutes.

Nutrition Information

- Calories: 254 calories;
- Total Carbohydrate: 26.3 g
- Cholesterol: 35 mg
- Total Fat: 9.7 g
- Protein: 16.4 g
- Sodium: 339 mg

58. Eggplant Pasta

"Quick and easy pasta dish!"
Serving: 8 | Prep: 15m | Ready in: 55m

Ingredients

- 1/4 cup olive oil
- 2 cloves garlic, minced
- 1 eggplant, peeled and cut into 1/2-inch cubes
- 1 (28 oz.) can plum tomatoes with juice, chopped
- 1 (16 oz.) package rigatoni pasta

Direction

- In a large skillet, heat the olive oil over medium heat. Cook while stirring garlic for 1-2 mins until fragrant. Put in eggplant; cook for about 5 mins until eggplant has softened, stirring constantly. Put in juice and tomatoes; cook for about 20 mins until the sauce is reduced slightly.
- Boil the lightly salted water in a large pot. In boiling water, cook the rigatoni for about 13 mins, until cooked through yet firm to bite, stirring occasionally. Drain, then place into the serving bowl.
- Add sauce over the pasta.

Nutrition Information

- Calories: 295 calories;
- Total Carbohydrate: 48.8 g
- Cholesterol: 0 mg
- Total Fat: 8.3 g
- Protein: 8.9 g
- Sodium: 145 mg

59. Eggplant Red Gravy With Anchovies

"This is a great New Orleans style gravy that you will surely enjoy."
Serving: 8 | Prep: 15m | Ready in: 1h15m

Ingredients

- 3 tbsps. olive oil
- 1 large onion, chopped
- 1 green bell pepper, seeded and cubed
- 3 cloves garlic, minced
- 1 pinch red pepper flakes (optional)
- 1/8 tsp. dried oregano
- 1 bay leaf
- 4 cups peeled, cubed eggplant
- 1 (16 oz.) can crushed Italian tomatoes, with liquid
- 1/4 cup tomato paste (optional)
- 2 cups sliced fresh mushrooms
- 1 1/2 (2 oz.) cans anchovies with capers, mashed
- salt and ground black pepper to taste
- 1 (16 oz.) package angel hair pasta
- 1/2 cup grated Parmesan cheese for topping

Direction

- Over medium heat, heat oil in a heavy saucepan. Put the bay leaf, oregano, red pepper flakes, garlic, bell pepper and onion and cook and stir until onion is tender.
- Mix in anchovies, mushrooms, tomato paste, tomatoes with liquid and eggplant and cover. Over low heat, simmer for about 30 minutes, until eggplant is tender, stirring frequently. Remove the lid when the eggplant is tender and cook until most of the liquid from the tomatoes has evaporated. Season it with pepper and salt to taste.
- While simmering the sauce, in a big pot, let lightly salted water boil. Put pasta and cook until tender for 4 minutes. Drain it and stir the

eggplant gravy in. Put parmesan cheese on top. Serve.

Nutrition Information

- Calories: 296 calories;
- Total Carbohydrate: 42.8 g
- Cholesterol: 12 mg
- Total Fat: 9.3 g
- Protein: 13.2 g
- Sodium: 643 mg

60. Enhanced Spaghetti

"Lift up your spaghetti with this way of cooking."
Serving: 8 | Prep: 1m | Ready in: 9m

Ingredients

- 1 gallon water
- 2 tbsps. paprika
- 1 tbsp. garlic powder
- 2 cubes beef bouillon
- 1 tsp. salt (optional)
- 1 (16 oz.) package uncooked spaghetti

Direction

- In a large pot, add water. Add salt, beef bouillon, garlic powder and paprika to season. Boil. Cook and stir spaghetti in boiling water in 4 minutes. Take away from the heat; set aside in 4 minutes with cover. Drain and rinse if desired, make sure not to overdo. Combine with your favorite sauce to serve.

Nutrition Information

- Calories: 218 calories;
- Total Carbohydrate: 43.7 g
- Cholesterol: < 1 mg
- Total Fat: 1.1 g
- Protein: 7.9 g
- Sodium: 525 mg

61. Farfalle With Asparagus And Smoked Salmon

"A light salad with only few ingredients for the summer!"
Serving: 4 | Prep: 10m | Ready in: 2h30m

Ingredients

- 1 (8 oz.) package farfalle pasta
- 1/2 cup fresh steamed asparagus tips
- 1 oz. smoked salmon, chopped
- 1 lemon, juiced
- 1 tbsp. chopped pistachio nuts
- 1 tsp. chopped fresh basil
- 1 tbsp. extra virgin olive oil
- salt and pepper to taste

Direction

- Cook pasta in salted boiling water to al dente in a large pot. Use cold water to rinse then drain.
- Steam asparagus over boiling water until it gets softened yet still firm. Drain well, let it cool and chop.
- Mix together pepper, salt, olive oil, basil, pistachios, lemon juice, smoked salmon, asparagus and pasta in a large bowl. Combine well and put into the refrigerator in 2 hours. Take it out, serve at room temperature.

Nutrition Information

- Calories: 261 calories;
- Total Carbohydrate: 45.1 g
- Cholesterol: 2 mg
- Total Fat: 6 g
- Protein: 10 g
- Sodium: 71 mg

62. Fettuccine With Garlic Herb Butter

"Add fresh herbs according to your tastes."
Serving: 4 | Prep: 10m | Ready in: 20m

Ingredients

- 6 oz. dry fettuccini pasta
- 1 tsp. butter
- 1 clove garlic, minced
- 1 tbsp. chopped fresh parsley
- 1 tbsp. chopped fresh basil
- 1 tbsp. chopped fresh marjoram (optional)
- 1 tbsp. chopped fresh thyme (optional)
- 1 tbsp. butter
- 1/8 tsp. salt
- 1 pinch ground black pepper

Direction

- Boil big pot of lightly salted water. Add pasta; cook till al dente for 8-10 minutes. Drain.
- Meanwhile, melt 1 tsp. butter in small saucepan on medium heat. Add garlic; cook till garlic starts to be golden for 30-60 seconds.
- Mix cooked garlic, ground black pepper, salt, 1 tbsp. butter, thyme, marjoram, basil and parsley well in small bowl. Toss with pasta; serve.

Nutrition Information

- Calories: 189 calories;
- Total Carbohydrate: 31.4 g
- Cholesterol: 10 mg
- Total Fat: 4.9 g
- Protein: 5.8 g
- Sodium: 103 mg

63. Fettuccini Alfredo II

"Garlicky and yummy."
Serving: 8

Ingredients

- 1 1/2 cups nonfat evaporated milk
- 10 cloves garlic
- 1 lb. dry fettuccine pasta
- 1/2 cup nonfat milk
- 1 tsp. cornstarch
- 2 tbsps. lowfat cream cheese
- 1/2 cup grated Parmesan cheese

Direction

- Heat and simmer garlic cloves and 1 1/2 cups evaporated milk in pan, for 15-20 minutes, till garlic is soft; milk will slightly reduce.
- Process cream cheese with garlic mixture and milk in a blender till smooth.
- Put mixture back in pan. Add cornstarch and 1/2 cup nonfat milk. Heat to simmer (sauce will slightly thicken), then add 1/4 cup of parmesan cheese.
- Boil big pot of lightly salted water. Add pasta; cook till al dente for 8-10 minutes. Drain. Toss cooked pasta with sauce then season with pepper and salt. Sprinkle parsley over. Serve leftover parmesan cheese separately.

Nutrition Information

- Calories: 284 calories;
- Total Carbohydrate: 49.5 g
- Cholesterol: 9 mg
- Total Fat: 3.6 g
- Protein: 14.3 g
- Sodium: 153 mg

64. Five Can Casserole

"Super simple!"
Serving: 6 | Prep: 10m | Ready in: 35m

Ingredients

- 1 (6 oz.) can chicken chunks, drained
- 1 (5 oz.) can evaporated milk
- 1 (10.75 oz.) can condensed cream of chicken soup
- 1 (10.75 oz.) can condensed cream of mushroom soup
- 1 (5 oz.) can chow mein noodles

Direction

- Start preheating oven to 350°F (175°C). Grease 2-qt casserole dish.
- In a mixing bowl, stir together noodles, cream of mushroom soup, cream of chicken soup, milk and chicken. Transfer to the prepared casserole dish. Bake for about 25 mins in the preheated oven, until bubbly and hot.

Nutrition Information

- Calories: 283 calories;
- Total Carbohydrate: 23.6 g
- Cholesterol: 28 mg
- Total Fat: 15 g
- Protein: 13.4 g
- Sodium: 1001 mg

65. Four Cheese Macaroni And Cheese

""A layered four cheese recipe that shared by a friend. I didn't like to cook and that was very easy to make. Now I prepare this dish every special occasion.""
Serving: 9 | Prep: 20m | Ready in: 40m

Ingredients

- 1/2 (8 oz.) package elbow macaroni
- 1 cup shredded sharp Cheddar cheese
- 1 cup shredded provolone cheese
- 1 cup shredded mozzarella cheese
- 1 cup shredded Colby-Monterey Jack cheese
- 1 egg, beaten
- 1 cup milk

Direction

- Place a lightly salted water in a large saucepan and make it boil. Add macaroni in the saucepan and cook for 8-10 minutes or until al dente; strain.
- Prepare the oven by preheating to 350°F (175°C). Prepare an 8x8-inch baking dish that is lightly greased.
- Then scatter the cheddar cheese over the bottom of the baking dish. Place a thin layer of macaroni on top. Put Provolone cheese on top of macaroni, one more layer of macaroni, a layer of mozzarella and third layer of macaroni. Layer Colby-Monterey jack cheese on top. Place the egg over all, next the milk.
- Place in the preheated oven and bake for 20 minutes or until golden brown and bubbly.

Nutrition Information

- Calories: 260 calories;
- Total Carbohydrate: 11.9 g
- Cholesterol: 69 mg
- Total Fat: 16.2 g
- Protein: 16.5 g
- Sodium: 420 mg

66. Fresh Zucchini Pasta Sauce

"This pasta dish is not only tasty but also simple to make! The pasta cooks the zucchini in its bowl."
Serving: 4 | Prep: 15m | Ready in: 1h15m

Ingredients

- 2 zucchini, grated
- 3 cloves garlic, minced
- 2 tbsps. olive oil
- salt to taste
- 1 (8 oz.) package angel hair pasta

Direction

- In a big bowl, mix together garlic and zucchini, stirring with salt and olive oil. Set the mixture aside for 1 hour until flavors blend.
- Boil a big pot of lightly salted water and cook angel hair, occasionally stirring, for 4-5 minutes until cooked through and firm to the bite. Drain then add with the zucchini mixture, tossing to blend and to cook the zucchini slightly.

Nutrition Information

- Calories: 239 calories;
- Total Carbohydrate: 35.1 g
- Cholesterol: 0 mg
- Total Fat: 8.4 g
- Protein: 7.3 g
- Sodium: 125 mg

67. Garden Basket Pasta With Clam Sauce

"Garden-fresh vegetables mixed with clams!"
Serving: 8

Ingredients

- 2 (6.5 oz.) cans minced clams
- 1 tbsp. olive oil
- 1/2 cup minced onion
- 1/2 cup minced carrots
- 6 cloves garlic, minced
- 2 cups chopped tomatoes
- 1/2 cup red bell pepper, chopped
- 1/2 tsp. salt
- 1/2 tsp. ground black pepper
- 1/4 tsp. crushed red pepper flakes
- 1/2 cup chopped fresh parsley
- 1/4 cup chopped fresh basil
- 1 lb. dry fettuccine pasta

Direction

- Strain clams and keep 1 cup of clam juice for later use; put clams aside.

- Heat oil over medium-high heat in a large non-stick skillet. Add garlic, carrot, and minced onion and sauté for 3 minutes; add in red/black pepper, salt, bell pepper, tomatoes, and reserved clam juice then bring to boil. Lower the heat and allow to simmer until thickened slightly or for 20 minutes.
- In a large pot, add lightly salted water then bring to a boil. Add pasta in and cook till al dente or for 8-10 minutes; strain. Remove sauce from heat, add in basil, parsley, and clams, and stir. Pour on pasta and toss gently.

Nutrition Information

- Calories: 289 calories;
- Total Carbohydrate: 49.1 g
- Cholesterol: 34 mg
- Total Fat: 3.8 g
- Protein: 15.8 g
- Sodium: 200 mg

68. Garlic Shrimp Linguine

"A dazzlingly delicious and simple recipe."
Serving: 8 | Prep: 10m | Ready in: 30m

Ingredients

- 1 lb. uncooked linguine
- 1 tbsp. butter
- 3 tbsps. white wine
- 2 tsps. grated Parmesan cheese
- 3 cloves garlic, minced
- 1 tsp. chopped fresh parsley
- 1 pinch salt and pepper to taste
- 1 lb. medium shrimp, peeled and deveined

Direction

- In a large pot, add lightly salted water then bring to a boil. Then add pasta and cook till al dente or for 8-10 minutes; strain.
- Melt butter over medium low heat in a medium-sized saucepan; stir in parsley, garlic, cheese, and wine, use pepper and salt for

seasoning. Simmer for 3-5 minutes over low heat, and frequently stir.

- Increase heat to medium high, in saucepan, add shrimp; cook till shrimp get pink or for about 3 to 4 minutes. Do not let shrimp get overcooked.
- Divide pasta into portions and pour sauce on top; use fresh parsley and Parmesan cheese for garnish, if needed.

Nutrition Information

- Calories: 287 calories;
- Total Carbohydrate: 42.3 g
- Cholesterol: 77 mg
- Total Fat: 4.9 g
- Protein: 17.6 g
- Sodium: 126 mg

69. Gorgonzola Cream Sauce

"Serve this with stuffed pasta, topped with diced apple and crunchy toasted walnuts."
Serving: 6 | Prep: 15m | Ready in: 40m

Ingredients

- 1 cup heavy whipping cream
- salt and freshly ground black pepper to taste
- 1 pinch cayenne pepper, or to taste
- 6 oz. dry miniature ravioli
- 3 oz. crumbled Gorgonzola cheese
- 2 tbsps. chopped Italian flat leaf parsley
- 2 tbsps. freshly grated Parmesan cheese
- 1/2 apple, diced
- 1/4 cup chopped toasted walnuts
- 1 tsp. chopped Italian flat leaf parsley

Direction

- Over medium heat, put a heavy skillet. Put cream into skillet, simmer, and allow cream cook for 8 minutes till it reduces by half, mixing from time to time. Season with cayenne pepper, black pepper and salt.
- Boil a pot of salted water. Into boiling water, put dried ravioli and cook, mixing from time

to time, for 16 to 18 minutes till pasta is tender. Drain the pasta, setting aside a cup of pasta water.

- Slowly fold cooked ravioli into cream sauce and set heat to low. Add in Gorgonzola cheese, mixing slowly till melted. Thin the sauce with a bit of pasta cooking water if sauce is too thick.
- Mix in Parmesan cheese and 2 tbsps. parsley. Put into a serving bowl and scatter 1 tsp. parsley, walnuts and diced apple over.

Nutrition Information

- Calories: 300 calories;
- Total Carbohydrate: 12.6 g
- Cholesterol: 82 mg
- Total Fat: 24.4 g
- Protein: 8.5 g
- Sodium: 258 mg

70. Greek Couscous

""A delectable Israeli couscous cooked Greek-style.""
Serving: 3 | Prep: 20m | Ready in: 45m

Ingredients

- 1/4 cup chicken broth
- 1/2 cup water
- 1 tsp. minced garlic
- 1/2 cup pearl (Israeli) couscous
- 1/4 cup chopped sun-dried tomatoes
- 1/4 cup sliced Kalamata olives
- 2 tbsps. crumbled feta cheese
- 1 cup canned garbanzo beans, rinsed and drained
- 1 tsp. dried oregano
- 1/2 tsp. ground black pepper
- 1 tbsp. white wine vinegar
- 1 1/2 tsps. lemon juice

Direction

- In a saucepan, put water, chicken broth and garlic; let it boil. Add in the couscous then cover and remove the pan from heat. Let the couscous soak in the water mixture for about 5 minutes until the liquid is completely absorbed. Use a fork to fluff the couscous. Let the couscous cool down until warm in temperature.

- In a big serving bowl, lightly mix the garbanzo beans, couscous, olives, sun-dried tomatoes and feta cheese. In a small bowl, combine white wine vinegar, lemon juice, oregano and black pepper and put it on top of the couscous mixture. Mix everything then serve.

Nutrition Information

- Calories: 254 calories;
- Total Carbohydrate: 42.4 g
- Cholesterol: 6 mg
- Total Fat: 5.6 g
- Protein: 9 g
- Sodium: 592 mg

71. Green Bean Orzo Pasta

"Healthy, a bit nutty, and easy pasta dish that you can pair with any meat. It's also really adaptable that you can add whatever you desire."
Serving: 8 | Prep: 15m | Ready in: 30m

Ingredients

- 1 1/2 cups orzo pasta
- 1 (12 oz.) bag fresh green beans, trimmed
- 3 tbsps. olive oil, divided
- 1/2 cup pine nuts, or more to taste
- 1 (14.5 oz.) can petite diced tomatoes, drained and rinsed
- 1/2 cup grated Parmesan cheese
- 1 tsp. dried basil
- salt and ground black pepper to taste

Direction

- Boil a big pot of lightly salted water; add orzo. Cook for about 11mins until completely cooked yet firm to chew, stir from time to time; drain.

- In a pot, put a steamer insert, then pour in water until just under the base of the steamer; boil. Put in green beans; steam for 2-4mins, covered, until tender.
- On medium-low heat, heat a tbsp. of olive oil in a pan; add pine nuts. Cook and stir for 2-4mins until aromatic and toasted.
- In a big bowl, mix pepper, salt, basil, Parmesan cheese, remaining olive oil, tomatoes, pine nuts, green beans and orzo together.

Nutrition Information

- Calories: 275 calories;
- Total Carbohydrate: 34.1 g
- Cholesterol: 4 mg
- Total Fat: 11.4 g
- Protein: 10.3 g
- Sodium: 161 mg

72. Greg's Special Rotini With Mushrooms

"This dish will wow your family."
Serving: 6 | Ready in: 10m

Ingredients

- 1 box Barilla® Pronto™ Rotini
- 1/2 cup Marsala cooking wine
- 1/2 cup Barilla® Mushroom Sauce
- 3/4 cup baby bella (crimini) mushrooms, sliced
- 1/2 cup grated pecorino cheese
- 2 tbsps. chopped fresh parsley
- Salt and black pepper to taste

Direction

- In a large skillet, add the whole pasta box (about 12-inch in diameter). Pour 2 1/2 cups cold water to skillet, making sure that pasta is covered with water. Put in wine and mushrooms. Turn burner to high, set timer to

10 minutes (optional: season to taste with a bit of salt).

- Cook on high until almost all liquid is evaporated, stirring occasionally.
- Put in sauce. Heat through gently, stirring to combine.
- Take away from the heat. Stir in parsley and cheese. Enjoy immediately.

Nutrition Information

- Calories: 287 calories;
- Total Carbohydrate: 47.8 g
- Cholesterol: 10 mg
- Total Fat: 3.8 g
- Protein: 11.2 g
- Sodium: 211 mg

73. Ham And Cheese Pasta Bake

"This dish will wow your family."
Serving: 8 | Prep: 10m | Ready in: 50m

Ingredients

- 1 (16 oz.) package rotini pasta
- 1 (26 oz.) jar onion and garlic spaghetti sauce
- 1 lb. thickly sliced honey baked ham, cut into 1/2 inch cubes
- 1 tsp. minced garlic
- 1 tsp. black pepper
- 1/2 tsp. onion powder
- 2 cups shredded mozzarella cheese
- 1/4 cup grated Parmesan cheese

Direction

- Start preheating the oven to 425°F (220°C).
- Combine pepper, onion powder, garlic, ham, spaghetti sauce and dry pasta in a large bowl. Fill water into sauce jar, then pour over the mixture. Mix well, then spoon into a casserole dish (9x13 inches). Tightly cover with foil.
- Bake for 35 mins in the preheated oven. Take off foil carefully. Sprinkle with Parmesan

cheese and mozzarella. Bake until cheese melts or 5 mins.

Nutrition Information

- Calories: 272 calories;
- Total Carbohydrate: 28.8 g
- Cholesterol: 46 mg
- Total Fat: 8 g
- Protein: 22.1 g
- Sodium: 1164 mg

74. Healthier Beef Stroganoff III

""If you're looking for a healthier version of Donna's classic stroganoff, this recipe is great. It makes use of less butter, light sour cream and fresh mushrooms, to be served with whole wheat noodles.""
Serving: 8 | Prep: 35m | Ready in: 1h35m

Ingredients

- 2 lbs. beef chuck roast
- 1/2 tsp. salt
- 1/2 tsp. ground black pepper
- 1 tbsp. butter
- 1/2 lb. white mushrooms, sliced
- 4 green onions, sliced (white and green parts)
- 2 tbsps. butter, divided
- 1/3 cup white wine
- 1/4 cup all-purpose flour
- 1 1/4 cups reduced-sodium beef stock, divided
- 1 tsp. prepared mustard
- 1/3 cup light sour cream
- salt and ground black pepper to taste

Direction

- Discard any fat and gristle from the roast and slice the meat up into 1/2-inch by 2-inch long strips. Sprinkle with 1/2 tsp. of salt and 1/2 tsp. of pepper to season.
- In a big skillet, melt 1 tbsp. of butter over medium heat then add the green onions and mushrooms. Cook for about 6 minutes until the mushrooms brown, stirring from time to

time. Transfer it to a bowl. Add 1 tbsp. of butter to the skillet. Cook and stir one half of the beef strips until browned for about 5 minutes, then move it to a bowl. Do the same for the remaining beef strips and butter until all are cooked. Deglaze the pan by pouring wine into the hot skillet and scraping up the browned pieces.

- In a jar with a tight fitting lid, shake 1/4 of beef broth together with flour until well combined. Whisk this into the skillet until smooth then stir in the mustard and remaining broth and transfer the beef back into the pan.

- Cover it up and let it simmer for about an hour until the meat becomes tender. About five minutes before serving, mix in the sour cream and prepped mushrooms and let it heat briefly. Sprinkle with salt and pepper to season.

Nutrition Information

- Calories: 256 calories;
- Total Carbohydrate: 6 g
- Cholesterol: 66 mg
- Total Fat: 17.9 g
- Protein: 16.4 g
- Sodium: 286 mg

75. Horizon Mac & Cheese

""The flavor and color added by steamed broccoli makes this child-satisfying mac 'n cheese. Yummy paired with your favorite orange smoothie and homemade meatballs!""
Serving: 4 | Prep: 10m | Ready in: 22m

Ingredients

- 1 (6 oz.) box Horizon® ClassicMac™ Macaroni & Mild Cheddar Cheese
- 1 tbsp. butter
- 1/2 cup shredded sharp Cheddar cheese
- 2 oz. Horizon® Organic Milk
- Cooked broccoli florets (optional)

Direction

- Cook noodles based on the package instructions.
- Strain and place into a big bowl.
- Instantly add the shredded cheese and butter. Whisk to mix while still hot. The cheese should dissolve. If it doesn't, place the mixture back into the pan and heat for 1 more minute on medium, constantly whisking until the cheese has dissolved.
- Put in the milk, cheese mix and broccoli if you want. Mix well until fully combined.

Nutrition Information

- Calories: 255 calories;
- Total Carbohydrate: 33 g
- Cholesterol: 25 mg
- Total Fat: 9.3 g
- Protein: 10.1 g
- Sodium: 482 mg

76. Hot Tomato Sauce

"Your family will definitely eat up this dish!"
Serving: 4 | Prep: 15m | Ready in: 30m

Ingredients

- 8 oz. dry pasta
- 1 fresh red chile pepper, chopped
- 1 red bell pepper, chopped
- 1 onion, chopped
- 1 (28 oz.) can diced tomatoes with juice
- 2 tbsps. tomato puree
- 2 tsps. chili powder

Direction

- Start preheating the oven to 300°F (150°C). Boil the lightly salted water in a large pot. Put in pasta. Cook until al dente or for 8 to 10 mins, then drain.
- In the meantime, sauté onion, bell pepper and chile pepper in large skillet until soft. Put in chili powder, puree and tomatoes. Cook for 2

mins longer. Using hand blender, puree into a smooth sauce or using a food processor, puree in batches.

- In a 9x13-inch baking dish, combine sauce and pasta. Bake for 15 mins. Enjoy hot.

Nutrition Information

- Calories: 283 calories;
- Total Carbohydrate: 52.4 g
- Cholesterol: 67 mg
- Total Fat: 2.9 g
- Protein: 10.8 g
- Sodium: 370 mg

77. Hot Wheels Pasta

"This summer pasta is easy to make."
Serving: 4 | Prep: 20m | Ready in: 45m

Ingredients

- 2 tbsps. olive oil
- 1/2 cup chopped green onions
- 1 anchovy fillet
- 3 cloves garlic, minced
- 2 zucchini - alternating strips of peel removed lengthwise and zucchini sliced
- salt and ground black pepper to taste
- 2 cups tomato sauce
- 3/4 cup chicken stock
- 1 pinch white sugar (optional)
- 1 cup seeded and sliced jalapeno peppers
- 1 cup seeded and sliced red Fresno chile peppers
- 1/2 cup seeded and sliced yellow mini bell pepper
- 1/2 cup seeded and sliced orange mini bell pepper
- 2 1/2 cups rotelle pasta
- 2 tbsps. chopped fresh flat-leaf parsley, divided
- 2 tsps. freshly grated Parmigiano-Reggiano cheese

Direction

- Boil the salted water in a large pot.
- Set the heavy pan over medium heat. In the hot pan, pour the olive oil. Put in anchovy fillet and green onions. Cook while stirring for 2-3 mins until green onions become tender and anchovy breaks down. Put garlic into skillet; cook for about one minute until translucent.
- Stir the zucchini into the green onion mixture. Cook for about 2 mins, until the zucchini slices begin to tender, stirring occasionally. Sprinkle with black pepper and salt; cook 1-2 mins more until the centers of zucchini begin to change to slightly green color.
- Pour chicken stock and tomato sauce into pan. Lower the heat to low; put in sugar. Mix orange mini pepper rings, yellow mini pepper, Fresno, and jalapeno into the mixture. Simmer sauce and lower the heat to low.
- Pour the rotelle pasta into the boiling water. Cook for about 7 mins, until the pasta is still firm slightly, stirring often. Drain and allow the pasta to stand for 2 mins.
- Boil sauce; mix in the rotelle pasta. Lower the heat to medium. Cook for 2-3 mins more, stirring often, until peppers, zucchini, and pasta are tender. Taste to adjust the levels of black pepper and salt. Mix in about 1 1/2 tsp. of the parsley. Serve in bowls. Add remaining half tsp. of parsley and Parmigiano-Reggiano cheese on top.

Nutrition Information

- Calories: 269 calories;
- Total Carbohydrate: 42.4 g
- Cholesterol: 2 mg
- Total Fat: 8.7 g
- Protein: 9.6 g
- Sodium: 876 mg

78. How To Make Turkey Manicotti

"Turn turkey leftovers to a tasty dish!"
Serving: 6 | Prep: 20m | Ready in: 2h25m

Ingredients

- Crepes:
- 2 eggs
- 3/4 cup all-purpose flour
- 3/4 cup water
- 1/2 tsp. salt
- 1/2 tsp. olive oil
- Filling:
- 1 cup diced cooked turkey
- 1 cup whole-milk ricotta cheese
- 1 egg
- 1/2 cup freshly shredded Parmigiano-Reggiano cheese
- 1/2 cup shredded mozzarella cheese
- 1/4 tsp. dried marjoram
- 1/8 tsp. red pepper flakes
- 1/4 cup chopped Italian parsley
- salt to taste
- 1 tsp. olive oil, or as needed
- 1 1/2 cups marinara sauce, divided
- 2 tsps. olive oil, divided
- 1/3 cup freshly shredded Parmigiano-Reggiano cheese
- 1 tbsp. freshly shredded Parmigiano-Reggiano cheese for garnish, or as desired
- 1 tbsp. chopped Italian parsley

Direction

- Start preheating the oven to 350°F (175°C).
- In a bowl, thoroughly whisk half tsp. of olive oil, salt, water, flour and 2 eggs together to create a very smooth batter. Cover the bowl in plastic wrap. Place the batter in refrigerator for 60 mins.
- In a bowl, mix a quarter cup of Italian parsley, red pepper flakes, marjoram, mozzarella cheese, half cup of the Parmigiano-Reggiano cheese, 1 egg, ricotta cheese and turkey until combined thoroughly. Season to taste with salt.
- Set a nonstick pan over medium-high heat; generously brush with one tsp. of the olive oil (as needed). Swirl about a quarter cup of the batter into bottom of pan, then tilt to make a thin pancake covering the skillet's bottom. Cook for 60-90 seconds until the crepe's bottom is dry. Turn the crepe over; cook for 60-90 more seconds until there are small browned spots on the other side. Do the same with the remaining batter to create six crepes. Arrange crepes onto a plate as you make them.
- Spread the bottom of a 9x12 inches baking dish with about half cup of the marinara sauce. Spread about half tsp. olive oil with a brush into a thin layer up the sides of dish. Arrange the crepe on the work surface, dimpled side down. Spread crepe with about 1/3 - 1/2 cup of the filling in a line down the center. Roll the crepe over the filling and if desired, tuck in ends. Lay the filled crepe into baking dish. Do the same with the remaining filling and crepes to create six manicotti.
- Spread the remaining one cup of the marinara sauce in a line onto manicotti down the crepe's center, covering center 1/3 of manicotti. Sprinkle all over the manicotti with 1/3 cup of the Parmigiano-Reggiano cheese. Drizzle the remaining 1 1/2 tsp. of the olive oil over manicotti.
- Bake in preheated oven for about 45 mins until the manicotti are puffy and browned slightly. Allow to stand to cool for 5 mins. Decorate with one tbsp. of the Parmigiano-Reggiano cheese or as preferred and one tbsp. of the Italian parsley, then serve.

Nutrition Information

- Calories: 286 calories;
- Total Carbohydrate: 21.6 g
- Cholesterol: 127 mg
- Total Fat: 13.1 g
- Protein: 19.6 g
- Sodium: 791 mg

79. Irresistible Healthy Vegetarian Stuffed Peppers

"Delicious and nutritious vegetarian pepper dish. You can freeze these easily for dinners or weekday lunches."
Serving: 12 | Prep: 30m | Ready in: 1h45m

Ingredients

- 8 oz. whole wheat orzo pasta
- 12 large orange bell peppers
- 2 tbsps. butter
- 1 tbsp. olive oil
- 10 cloves garlic, thinly sliced
- 1 (8 oz.) package sliced fresh white mushrooms
- 1 (8 oz.) package sliced cremini mushrooms
- 2 tbsps. balsamic vinegar
- 1 (28 oz.) can diced Italian paste tomatoes (such as San Marzano)
- 1 (14 oz.) can whole Italian paste tomatoes (such as San Marzano), drained and torn into large chunks
- 1 cup shredded mozzarella cheese
- 1 zucchini, shredded
- 1/2 cup grated Parmesan cheese
- 8 cloves garlic, minced
- 2 tbsps. dried oregano
- 2 tbsps. torn fresh basil leaves
- 2 tsps. red pepper flakes
- salt and ground black pepper to taste
- 4 cups vegetable broth
- 3/4 cup grated Parmesan cheese, divided

Direction

- Boil a big pot of lightly salted water. Let the orzo cook in the boiling water for about 8 minutes, mixing from time to time, until completely cooked but firm to chew; drain. Move the orzo to a big bowl.
- Preheat the oven to 200°C or 400°F.
- Slice an inch from the orange bell peppers' tops; get rid of the tops and remove the seeds from the peppers. Place the peppers in a roasting pan in an upright position, then tightly fit the peppers so that it will stay in place.
- Melt the olive oil and butter on medium-low heat; add 10 cloves of garlic and let it cook in the hot butter mixture for about 8 minutes, until the garlic turns golden brown. Mix balsamic vinegar and cremini and white mushrooms into the garlic; cook and stir for around 10 minutes, until the mushrooms are soft. Drain the liquid, then combine the garlic and mushrooms into the orzo.
- Stir black pepper, salt, red pepper flakes, basil, oregano, 8 garlic cloves, half cup Parmesan cheese, zucchini, mozzarella cheese, torn whole tomatoes and diced tomatoes and their juice into the orzo mixture, then stuff it into the bell peppers. Pour the vegetable broth into the base of a roasting pan; use aluminum foil to cover the pan tightly.
- Bake for about 50 minutes in the preheated oven, until the filling is completely cooked, and the peppers are tender. Take off the foil, then sprinkle 1 tbsp. of Parmesan cheese on each pepper. Put it back into the oven and let it bake for about 15 minutes more, until the Parmesan cheese on top is bubbly and golden.

Nutrition Information

- Calories: 232 calories;
- Total Carbohydrate: 30.4 g
- Cholesterol: 18 mg
- Total Fat: 8 g
- Protein: 12.5 g
- Sodium: 508 mg

80. Japchae

"Healthy and authentic Korean recipe."
Serving: 8 | Prep: 30m | Ready in: 45m

Ingredients

- Sauce:
- 3 tbsps. soy sauce
- 2 1/2 tbsps. white sugar

- 2 tbsps. sesame oil
- 2 tsps. minced garlic
- Stir Fry Ingredients:
- 8 oz. sweet potato noodles
- 4 oz. lean beef, cut into 2-inch long strips
- 6 oz. fresh spinach
- salt and ground black pepper to taste
- 1 tbsp. vegetable oil, divided
- 1 small sweet onion, thinly sliced
- 4 mushrooms, stemmed and sliced
- 1 small carrot, cut into matchsticks

Direction

- In a bowl, mix garlic, sesame oil, sugar, and soy sauce until sugar melts into sauce.
- Boil a big pot of lightly salted water. In boiling water, cook sweet potato noodles for 6-7 minutes, occasionally stirring until firm to the bite but cooked through. Rinse noodles in cold water then drain. Place noodles in a bowl, add 2 tbsps. of sauce, then toss until coated.
- Squeeze beef in running water until juices are clear. Mix 1 tbsp. sauce and beef in a bowl together.
- Boil a pot of water. In boiling water, cook spinach for 1 minutes until wilted. Quickly drain and place spinach in a bowl with cold water to stop cooking process. Squeeze extra water out of spinach. Place in a big bowl. Season with pepper and salt.
- In a big skillet, heat 1 tbsp. oil on medium-high heat. Cook onion for 1-2 minutes until crisp and fragrant. Place onion in bowl with the spinach. In the same skillet, heat another 1 tsp. of oil. Cook mushrooms in hot oil for 1-2 minutes until light brown and still firm. Add into onion mixture. Heat leftover 1 tsp. of oil in the skillet. Cook carrot in hot oil for 1-2 minutes until crisp and light brown. Add to the onion mixture.
- Sauté beef for 1-2 minutes in the same skillet until its brown. Add into onion mixture. Stir and cook noodles for 1-2 minutes in the same skillet until they're heated through. Add to onion-beef mixture. Add leftover sauce on

noodles-beef mixture. Coat by tossing with your hands.

Nutrition Information

- Calories: 201 calories;
- Total Carbohydrate: 31.5 g
- Cholesterol: 7 mg
- Total Fat: 7 g
- Protein: 3.6 g
- Sodium: 368 mg

81. Johnny Marzetti II

""Adaptable dish and you can modify it based on your taste preference! Add another can if you enjoy kidney beans. Alternate one small can sliced black olives and a (4 oz.) can sliced mushrooms for the beans if you don't enjoy kidney beans.""
Serving: 20

Ingredients

- 1 lb. lean ground beef
- 1 lb. ground pork
- 1/4 cup butter
- 1 onion, chopped
- 1 cup chopped green bell pepper
- 1 cup chopped celery
- 1 (28 oz.) can stewed tomatoes, with liquid
- 1 (15 oz.) can kidney beans
- 2 tsps. salt
- 1 (16 oz.) package macaroni
- 1/2 cup grated Parmesan cheese

Direction

- In a large pot of boiling water, cook pasta until done. Strain.
- Stir-fry green pepper, celery and onion in butter or margarine in a large skillet until tender. Stir in the pork and ground beef and cook until meat is done. Strain well.
- Mix with pasta, salt, beans and stewed tomatoes. Transfer the mixture into two 9x13-inch baking pans and spread evenly. Place 1 cup of cheese on top of each pan.

- Place in the oven and bake for 30-35 minutes at 350°F.

Nutrition Information

- Calories: 264 calories;
- Total Carbohydrate: 23.5 g
- Cholesterol: 41 mg
- Total Fat: 12.9 g
- Protein: 13.2 g
- Sodium: 446 mg

82. Kaese Spaetzle

"A delicious homemade pasta with cheese and onion."
Serving: 8 | Prep: 10m | Ready in: 1h

Ingredients

- 1 1/2 cups all-purpose flour
- 3/4 tsp. ground nutmeg
- 3/4 tsp. salt
- 1/8 tsp. pepper
- 3 eggs
- 3/8 cup 2% milk
- 3 tbsps. butter
- 1 onion, sliced
- 1 1/2 cups shredded Emmentaler cheese

Direction

- Sift together pepper, salt, nutmeg and flour. In a medium bowl, whisk the eggs. Alternately stir in milk and flour mixture till smooth. Let sit for half an hour.
- Boil a big pot of slightly salted water. Press batter through a spaetzle press into the water. Alternatively, use a cheese grater, colander or a potato ricer. Once spaetzle has risen to surface of the water, transfer it to a bowl using a slotted spoon. Stir in a cup of cheese.
- In a big skillet, melt butter over medium-high heat. Put in onion, and cook till golden. Mix in the rest of the cheese and the spaetzle till well incorporated. Take away from heat, and serve right away.

Nutrition Information

- Calories: 245 calories;
- Total Carbohydrate: 20.1 g
- Cholesterol: 102 mg
- Total Fat: 13.1 g
- Protein: 11.5 g
- Sodium: 377 mg

83. Kellie's Simple Penne With Pepperoni And Cheese

"Combine fresh basil, pecorino with garlic, pepperoni and diced onions for a perfect penne pasta recipe."
Serving: 10 | Ready in: 6m

Ingredients

- 1 box Barilla® Pronto™ Penne
- 1 1/2 cups chicken broth
- 1 cup diced yellow onion
- 1 cup diced pepperoni
- 1 clove garlic, minced
- 1/2 cup grated pecorino cheese
- 5 basil leaves, torn
- Salt and black pepper to taste

Direction

- In a large skillet (about 12 inches in diameter), add full box of pasta. Pour in chicken broth and 1 1/2 cups of cold water so that the pasta is fully covered. Put onion in; higher the heat of the burner to high; set to 10 minutes on the timer (taste with a bit of salt if desired). Let it cook on high heat with occasional stirs until almost all of the liquid evaporates.
- When the pasta is nearly cooked, put in garlic and pepperoni; cook through gently.
- Take away from the heat; add basil and cheese, stir well. Ready for immediate serve.

Nutrition Information

- Calories: 253 calories;
- Total Carbohydrate: 27.3 g
- Cholesterol: 27 mg

- Total Fat: 11.3 g
- Protein: 10.6 g
- Sodium: 571 mg

84. Korean Sweet Potato Noodles (japchae)

"It's so satisfying."
Serving: 6 | Prep: 25m | Ready in: 1h25m

Ingredients

- Steak Marinade:
- 1/4 cup soy sauce
- 4 tsps. mirin (Japanese sweet wine)
- 1 tbsp. sesame oil
- 2 cloves garlic, minced
- 1 tsp. ground black pepper
- 1 lb. flank steak, sliced across the grain
- Noodle Sauce:
- 1/4 tbsp. soy sauce
- 2 tbsps. honey
- 1 tbsp. sesame oil
- 1 pinch ground black pepper
- 8 oz. Korean sweet potato noodles (dangmyun)
- 1 egg
- 2 cups baby spinach, or more to taste
- 1 tsp. light olive oil
- 1 large carrot, cut into matchsticks
- 1/2 onion, sliced

Direction

- In a bowl, combine one tsp. of pepper, garlic, one tbsp. of the sesame oil, mirin and a quarter cup of soy sauce. Put in steak; coat by stirring. Marinate at least half an hour.
- In a large bowl, combine one pinch pepper, one tbsp. of the sesame oil, honey and a quarter cup of soy sauce, then stir well.
- Bring a large pot of water to a rolling boil, then stir in the noodles; return to boil. Cook uncovered for about 5 mins, stirring occasionally, then drain. Put noodles into the sauce; coat by tossing.
- In a bowl, whisk egg. Over medium-low heat, heat a pan; pour in egg. Cook for about one minute each side, until firm. Cut into strips.
- Boil the lightly salted water in a large pot. Put in spinach. Cook, uncovered, for about one minute just until bright green, then drain in colander; immerse in the ice water for several minutes immediately to stop cooking process. Drain.
- In a large skillet, heat the olive oil over medium-high heat. Put in onion and carrot; sauté for about 5 mins until tender. Stir in marinade and steak; cook for 5-8 mins, until tender. Stir in the spinach. Put in egg and noodles; cook while stirring for about 2 mins until heated through and well combined.

Nutrition Information

- Calories: 283 calories;
- Total Carbohydrate: 33 g
- Cholesterol: 48 mg
- Total Fat: 9.9 g
- Protein: 14.2 g
- Sodium: 910 mg

85. Lasagna Cupcakes

"It's a yummy treat!"
Serving: 12 | Prep: 15m | Ready in: 45m

Ingredients

- cooking spray
- 1/3 lb. ground beef
- salt and ground black pepper to taste
- 24 wonton wrappers
- 1 3/4 cups grated Parmesan cheese
- 1 3/4 cups shredded mozzarella cheese
- 3/4 cup ricotta cheese
- 1 cup pasta sauce (such as Muir Glen®)
- 1/4 cup chopped fresh basil, or to taste (optional)

Direction

- Start preheating the oven to 375°F (190°C). Prepare the muffin cups with the cooking spray.
- Over medium-high heat, heat a large pan. In the hot skillet, cook while stirring beef for 5-7 mins until crumbly and browned; season with salt and pepper. Drain and remove the grease from beef.
- Cut the wonton wrappers with the biscuit cutter into 2 1/4 in. circles. Press 1 wonton into bottom per muffin cup. Sprinkle into each muffin cup with even amounts of ricotta cheese, mozzarella cheese, and Parmesan cheese. Add even amounts of the pasta sauce and ground beef on top of each portion.
- Split half cup of Parmesan cheese, half cup of mozzarella cheese, 1/2 ricotta cheese, half ground beef mixture and half cup of the pasta sauce between muffin cups and then layer, respectively, atop the wonton wrapper. Repeat the layering with the remaining wonton wrappers, half cup of Parmesan cheese, half cup of mozzarella cheese, the remaining ricotta cheese, the remaining ground beef, and the remaining pasta sauce. Add the remaining mozzarella cheese and Parmesan cheese on top of 'cupcakes'.
- Bake in the preheated oven for 18-20 mins until the 'cupcakes' edges have browned. Allow to cook for 5 mins in tins, then loosen the edges by running knife around the cupcakes edges to remove. Decorate with the fresh basil. Enjoy.

Nutrition Information

- Calories: 180 calories;
- Total Carbohydrate: 13.1 g
- Cholesterol: 30 mg
- Total Fat: 8.3 g
- Protein: 12.6 g
- Sodium: 477 mg

86. Lasagna Muffins

"This salad is colorful and flavorful!"
Serving: 12 | Prep: 15m | Ready in: 35m

Ingredients

- cooking spray
- 1 cup shredded mozzarella cheese
- 1 cup grated Asiago cheese
- 2 cups prepared pasta sauce
- 1/2 (16 oz.) package wonton wrappers

Direction

- Preheat oven to 375°F (190°C). Spray cooking spray over 12 muffin cups.
- In a bowl, combine Asiago cheese and mozzarella cheese together. Press into bottom of each muffin cup the wonton wrapper. Spoon the pasta sauce in every muffin cup, about halfway full; sprinkle 2-3 tbsps. cheese mixture over. Press the top of cheese layer with another wonton wrapper. Put in another spoonful of the sauce; sprinkle cheese on top. Repeat to fill all muffin cups.
- Bake in preheated oven for 20-25 minutes until cheese melts and sauce is bubbling.

Nutrition Information

- Calories: 147 calories;
- Total Carbohydrate: 16.8 g
- Cholesterol: 17 mg
- Total Fat: 5.5 g
- Protein: 7.1 g
- Sodium: 445 mg

87. Lazy Perogies

"It's just so delicious!"
Serving: 12 | Prep: 30m | Ready in: 1h40m

Ingredients

- 9 uncooked lasagna noodles

- 4 large baking potatoes, peeled and cut into 1-inch chunks
- 1/2 cup milk
- 1 tbsp. butter
- 1 tsp. onion salt, or to taste
- salt and black pepper to taste
- 1 cup shredded Cheddar cheese
- 1 lb. bacon
- 1 onion, chopped
- 2 cups dry cottage cheese
- 1 egg
- 1 tsp. onion salt, or to taste

Direction

- Bring the lightly salted water in a large pot to a rolling boil. Stir in lasagna noodles when water is boiling, about 3-4 at a time. Bring back to a boil. Cook noodles, uncovered, for about 10 mins each batch until pasta is cooked through yet still firm to bite, stirring occasionally. In a colander set in sink, drain it well. While you finish cooking the rest of noodles, lay cooked noodles flat on aluminum foil or waxed paper.
- Start preheating the oven to 350°F (175°C). Grease a 9x11 inches baking dish.
- In a large pot, put potatoes; add water to cover. Boil over high heat. Lower the heat to medium-low, simmer, covered, for about 20 mins until tender. Drain and let steam dry for 1-2 mins. Mash potatoes with potato masher with the butter and milk until they become smooth. Stir in one tsp. onion salt. Season with pepper and salt. Put mashed potatoes aside and let cool. Mix with the shredded Cheddar cheese once cooled.
- In a large, deep pan, put bacon. Cook for about 10 mins over medium-high heat, until almost crisp and evenly browned, turning occasionally. Put onion into hot bacon fat. Cook while stirring for about 8 mins until onion is translucent. Break bacon with a spatula or spoon into pieces. Put onion and bacon aside. In a bowl, mix one tsp. onion salt, egg and cottage cheese.
- For casserole, in prepared baking dish, put three lasagna noodles. Spread cottage cheese mixture over in an even layer. Add 3 more lasagna noodles on top of cottage cheese. Spread with the potato-cheese mixture in a layer. Place 3 more noodles on top of mashed potato layer. Spread top of casserole with bacon and onion in an even layer.
- Cover casserole with aluminum foil. Bake in preheated oven for about half an hour until casserole is hot and cheese melts. Let it set for about 10 mins, then serve.

Nutrition Information

- Calories: 271 calories;
- Total Carbohydrate: 27.6 g
- Cholesterol: 46 mg
- Total Fat: 10.4 g
- Protein: 16.9 g
- Sodium: 689 mg

88. Leftover Special Casserole

"A dish that came together from lots of ingredients left over."
Serving: 6 | Prep: 15m | Ready in: 45m

Ingredients

- 4 cups uncooked egg noodles
- 1 (10 oz.) package frozen mixed peas and carrots, thawed
- 1 small onion, minced
- 2 cups cooked ham, diced
- 1 (10.75 oz.) can condensed cream of mushroom soup
- 1/2 cup milk
- salt and pepper to taste

Direction

- Preheat the oven to 175 °C or 350 °F. Slightly oil a 9x13-inch baking dish. Boil a big pot of water. Put in the egg noodles, and cook till done, about 8 to 10 minutes; drain.

- In prepped baking dish, layer noodles, mixed peas and carrots, onions and ham. Combine the milk and soup, then add the mixture on top of casserole. Add pepper and salt to season, then press using back of fork to help soup mixture to seep through the casserole layers.
- Bake for half an hour at 175 °C or 350 °F, or till hot and bubbly.

Nutrition Information

- Calories: 239 calories;
- Total Carbohydrate: 28.4 g
- Cholesterol: 42 mg
- Total Fat: 8.8 g
- Protein: 12.4 g
- Sodium: 880 mg

89. Lemon Orzo Primavera

"This orzo dish with different vegetables, thyme, and lemon is perfect for picnics. To lessen the prep time, you can just chop the carrot and zucchini instead of grating the vegetables. Make sure to cook them a bit longer prior to adding the orzo."
Serving: 4 | Prep: 15m | Ready in: 30m

Ingredients

- 1 tbsp. olive oil
- 1 cup uncooked orzo pasta
- 1 clove garlic, crushed
- 1 medium zucchini, shredded
- 1 medium carrot, shredded
- 1 (14 oz.) can vegetable broth
- 1 lemon, zested
- 1 tbsp. chopped fresh thyme
- 1/4 cup grated Parmesan cheese

Direction

- In a pot, heat the oil on medium heat. Mix in orzo and let it cook for 2 minutes, until it turns golden. Mix in carrot, zucchini and garlic and let it cook for 2 minutes. Stir in lemon zest and pour in the broth; boil. Lower the heat to low

and let it simmer for 10 minutes, until the orzo becomes tender and the liquid is absorbed. Sprinkle thyme to season and put Parmesan on top, then serve.

Nutrition Information

- Calories: 279 calories;
- Total Carbohydrate: 44.7 g
- Cholesterol: 4 mg
- Total Fat: 6.3 g
- Protein: 10.4 g
- Sodium: 295 mg

90. Lighter Lasagna

"This dish will wow your family."
Serving: 8 | Prep: 15m | Ready in: 1h45m

Ingredients

- 1 (10 oz.) package frozen chopped spinach, thawed and drained
- 1 cup low-fat cottage cheese
- 1 egg
- cooking spray
- 1 onion, chopped
- 2 large garlic cloves, minced
- 2 cups chopped mushrooms
- 1 cup shredded carrots
- 1 lb. ground turkey breast
- 1 (26 oz.) jar low-fat pasta sauce (such as Healthy Request®)
- 1 cup water
- 1 tsp. dried rosemary, crushed
- 1 tsp. dried oregano
- 1 tsp. dried basil
- 6 no-boil lasagna noodles
- 1 cup shredded low-fat mozzarella cheese
- 1 cup tomato-vegetable juice cocktail

Direction

- Start preheating the oven to 400°F (200°C). In a large bowl, mix egg, cottage cheese and spinach.

- Set a large pan over medium-high heat. Coat with the nonstick cooking spray. Cook carrot, mushrooms, garlic and onion for about 5 mins until onion is soft. Put in ground turkey; stir for about 5 mins until cooked through. Pour water and pasta sauce into skillet. Season with basil, oregano and rosemary. Simmer the sauce for 10 mins.
- Spray nonstick cooking spray over 9x13 baking pan. Spread bottom of pan with 1/3 sauce. Add 3 noodles on top. Spoon on noodles with 1/3 more sauce. Add spinach mixture on top. Sprinkle half mozzarella cheese over. Top with the rest of the sauce and remaining 3 noodles. Evenly pour vegetable juice over lasagna. Add the remaining mozzarella on top. Cover the dish with foil.
- Bake for 45 mins in preheated oven. Discard the foil. Bake for 10 more mins. Take off from the oven; allow lasagna to rest for 10-15 mins. Serve!

Nutrition Information

- Calories: 263 calories;
- Total Carbohydrate: 24 g
- Cholesterol: 74 mg
- Total Fat: 9.2 g
- Protein: 25.4 g
- Sodium: 663 mg

91. Linguine With Fresh Sage-caper Sauce

"This dish is versatile."
Serving: 2 | Prep: 15m | Ready in: 45m

Ingredients

- 1 1/2 tsps. olive oil
- 2 cloves garlic, minced
- 1 (14.4 oz.) can whole peeled tomatoes, with liquid, quartered
- 2 tbsps. drained capers
- 2 bay leaves
- 1 pinch dried thyme leaves

- 1 1/2 tsps. thinly sliced fresh sage leaves
- 1/2 (8 oz.) package linguine pasta
- salt and pepper to taste

Direction

- In a saucepan, heat olive oil over medium heat. Mix in garlic. Cook for about 3 mins until fragrant. Stir in thyme leaves, bay leaves, capers and tomatoes. Bring to a simmer. Lower the heat to medium-low, keep simmering for 15 mins. Mix in the sage leaves. Simmer for 10 more mins.
- Boil the lightly salted water in a large pot. Put in pasta. Cook until al dente or for 8 to 10 mins, then drain. Put back to pot off of the heat. Season sauce to taste with pepper and salt. Pour over pasta; coat by tossing.

Nutrition Information

- Calories: 276 calories;
- Total Carbohydrate: 50.9 g
- Cholesterol: 0 mg
- Total Fat: 5.3 g
- Protein: 9.5 g
- Sodium: 551 mg

92. Linguine With Portobello Mushrooms

"Try to use fresh herbs."
Serving: 8 | Prep: 15m | Ready in: 45m

Ingredients

- 4 portobello mushroom caps
- 2 tbsps. extra virgin olive oil
- 1 lb. linguine pasta
- 1 tsp. red wine vinegar
- 1 tsp. chopped fresh oregano
- 1 tsp. chopped fresh basil
- 1/2 tsp. chopped fresh rosemary
- 2 cloves garlic, peeled and crushed
- 2 tsps. lemon juice
- salt and pepper to taste

Direction

- Preheat oven broiler.
- Boil big pot of lightly salted water. Add linguine; cook till al dente or for 9-13 minutes. Drain.
- Brush 1/2 of the olive oil on mushrooms; put on a medium baking sheet. In the prepped oven, broil for 6-8 minutes till tender and browned, frequently turning.
- Slice the mushrooms into 1/4-in. slices; put in a medium bowl. Mix with lemon juice, garlic, rosemary, basil, oregano, red wine vinegar and leftover olive oil; season with pepper and salt.
- Toss mushroom mixture and cooked linguine together in a big bowl.

Nutrition Information

- Calories: 250 calories;
- Total Carbohydrate: 44.6 g
- Cholesterol: 0 mg
- Total Fat: 4.8 g
- Protein: 9 g
- Sodium: 152 mg

93. Low Fat Cheesy Spinach And Eggplant Lasagna

" "It's a new lasagna recipe that is filled with lots of cheese and vegetables." "
Serving: 12 | Prep: 40m | Ready in: 1h25m

Ingredients

- 12 whole wheat lasagna noodles, dry
- 1 tsp. olive oil
- 2 tbsps. olive oil
- 3 cloves garlic, minced
- 1 eggplant, cubed
- 1 (28 oz.) can Italian herb-flavored tomato sauce
- 1 cup part-skim ricotta cheese
- 1 cup low-fat cottage cheese
- 1 cup shredded part-skim mozzarella cheese
- 1/4 cup shredded Parmesan cheese
- 1/2 tsp. salt
- 1/2 tsp. ground black pepper
- 1 egg
- 2 1/2 cups frozen chopped spinach, thawed and squeezed dry

Direction

- Heat the oven beforehand at a temperature of 375°F (190°C).
- Boil a large pot that is filled with water.
- Cook the lasagna noodles into the boiling water for 8 minutes until the noodles are al dente. Be sure to add 1 tsp. of oil into the water before cooking.
- Let the noodles drain and cool.
- In a large saucepan, warm at least 2 tbsp. of olive oil over a moderate heat.
- Sauté the eggplant chunks and garlic for 7 minutes, enough until the eggplant chunks were lightly cooked.
- Stir in tomato sauce and bring into simmer for 10-15 minutes until the eggplant is soft.
- In a clean bowl, whisk together the salt, egg, black pepper, mozzarella cheese, ricotta cheese, Parmesan cheese and the cottage cheese
- Stir in spinach into the mixture.
- In a 9x12-in. baking pan, layer the tomato sauce mixture.
- On top of it, arrange the four noodles, overlapping it if needed.
- Spread 1/3 of the remaining tomato sauce on the noodles.
- Top the tomato sauce with 1/3 of the ricotta mixture.
- Repeat same steps and layers twice, starting from layering the noodles followed by the sauce and ricotta mixture.
- End it by placing mozzarella cheese on its top.
- Let it bake in the preheated oven for about 45-60 minutes just until the mozzarella cheese topping is already light brown and the ricotta filling is all fixed.

Nutrition Information

- Calories: 206 calories;
- Total Carbohydrate: 23.2 g
- Cholesterol: 31 mg
- Total Fat: 7.6 g
- Protein: 13.7 g
- Sodium: 660 mg

94. Mac And Cheese I

"Try this and you will love it!"
Serving: 4 | Prep: 5m | Ready in: 43m

Ingredients

- 2 cups macaroni
- 1/2 cup nonfat cottage cheese
- 1 egg white
- 1/2 packet artificial sweetener
- 1/4 cup reduced fat processed cheese food, cubed
- 1/4 cup lowfat buttermilk
- 1/4 tsp. liquid smoke flavoring
- 1/2 cup crushed saltine crackers

Direction

- In a large pot, cook pasta in the boiling salted water until al dente. Grease a 2-qt. casserole dish.
- In a food processor, blend cottage cheese until smooth.
- Combine liquid smoke, buttermilk, cheese food, sweetener, egg white and cottage cheese in large bowl until mixed well. Stir in the pasta. Transfer to the prepared dish. Add crushed crackers on top.
- Bake for half an hour at 400°F (205°C).

Nutrition Information

- Calories: 291 calories;
- Total Carbohydrate: 48.9 g
- Cholesterol: 6 mg
- Total Fat: 3.4 g
- Protein: 14.9 g

- Sodium: 412 mg

95. Macaroni And Cheese II

""A super cheesy recipe and a great one at that! Decorate with fresh mint and carrot flowers for an attractive presentation.'"
Serving: 8

Ingredients

- 2 (11 oz.) cans condensed cream of Cheddar cheese soup
- 1 3/8 cups milk
- 2 tsps. prepared mustard
- 1/4 tsp. ground black pepper
- 3 cups rotini pasta
- 2 tbsps. bread crumbs
- 1 tbsp. butter, melted

Direction

- In a big pot of boiling salted water, put the pasta and cook until al dente. Strain. Mix in a large bowl the pepper, mustard, milk and condensed soup. Mix in macaroni. Place the mixture into a 2-qt.casserole that is greased. Mix in a cup the dissolved margarine or butter and bread crumbs. Then dust over macaroni mixture.
- Bake in the oven for 25 minutes at 400°F (205°C), or until bubbling and hot.

Nutrition Information

- Calories: 210 calories;
- Total Carbohydrate: 24.9 g
- Cholesterol: 25 mg
- Total Fat: 9.2 g
- Protein: 7.7 g
- Sodium: 623 mg

96. Manicotti Pancakes I

"It's so luscious!"
Serving: 6 | Prep: 5m | Ready in: 15m

Ingredients

- 1 cup all-purpose flour
- 4 eggs
- 1 tbsp. olive oil
- 1 tsp. salt
- 1 cup water

Direction

- In a medium bowl, combine water, salt, olive oil, eggs and flour. Stir until they become smooth. Over medium-high heat, heat a 7 inches pan, brush with olive oil lightly. Ladle into pan with enough batter to cover bottom. Cook about 30 seconds until bottom is brown and top is set. Lift the pancake onto the parchment paper; repeat. Fill the pancake with cheese filling or meat, add tomato sauce on top and bake.

Nutrition Information

- Calories: 161 calories;
- Total Carbohydrate: 16.2 g
- Cholesterol: 134 mg
- Total Fat: 7.6 g
- Protein: 6.7 g
- Sodium: 457 mg

97. Manicotti Pancakes II

"This awesome dish is from an old Italian family."
Serving: 12 | Prep: 5m | Ready in: 15m

Ingredients

- 3 eggs
- 1 cup milk
- 1 cup all-purpose flour

Direction

- In a big bowl, whip milk and eggs. Whip in flour till batter becomes smooth in texture. Use cooking spray to coat slightly a crepe pan or one 8-inch skillet over medium high heat. Drop a big spoonful of batter on pan to make one pancake at a time; tilt to cover the entire surface of the pan equally. Cook for roughly 2 minutes for each pancake, flipping once, till it turns golden in color.

Nutrition Information

- Calories: 66 calories;
- Total Carbohydrate: 9 g
- Cholesterol: 48 mg
- Total Fat: 1.7 g
- Protein: 3.3 g
- Sodium: 26 mg

98. Manti (turkish 'ravioli' With Yogurt Sauce)

""I love how warm the flavors of this traditional Turkish dish are. I like serving it in winter! You can use the Manti pasta if you want it to be like the traditional one. You can purchase such at any online Turkish store.""
Serving: 4 | Prep: 10m | Ready in: 20m

Ingredients

- 1 tsp. salt
- 1 tsp. dried mint
- 1 (9 oz.) package beef ravioli
- 1/4 cup butter
- 1 tsp. sweet paprika
- 1 tbsp. minced garlic
- 1 (8 oz.) container plain whole milk yogurt

Direction

- Boil a large pot of water. Stir in ravioli, mint, and salt. Let it cook for 3-5 minutes until the ravioli floats on top. Drain and keep warm.
- Meanwhile, place butter in a small saucepan and melt it over low heat. Mix in paprika.

Keep it warm while waiting for the ravioli. Add garlic into the yogurt.

- Arrange the drained ravioli into the plates or serving platter. Top the ravioli with yogurt, and then ladle the paprika butter over its top.

Nutrition Information

- Calories: 293 calories;
- Total Carbohydrate: 26.7 g
- Cholesterol: 60 mg
- Total Fat: 17.1 g
- Protein: 9.4 g
- Sodium: 1098 mg

well. Put the filling through a grinder until turns smooth (or use a food processor to puree until becomes smooth).

- Store the filling inside the refrigerator for up to 4 days or up to 3 months in the freezer.

Nutrition Information

- Calories: 107 calories;
- Total Carbohydrate: 1.6 g
- Cholesterol: 33 mg
- Total Fat: 8.2 g
- Protein: 6.5 g
- Sodium: 124 mg

99. Meat And Spinach Ravioli Filling

"This was made by my grandma when I was a kid. From an old recipe book."
Serving: 15 | Prep: 15m | Ready in: 40m

Ingredients

- 1 lb. ground beef
- 1 1/2 cups fresh spinach
- 5 tbsps. grated Parmesan cheese
- 1 1/4 tbsps. dried parsley
- 1/4 cup bread crumbs
- 1/4 cup olive oil
- 1 large egg
- 1/2 tsp. garlic salt
- 1 pinch black pepper

Direction

- Place a large skillet on the stove and turn to medium-high heat then put in the ground beef. Stir and cook until the beef is equally brown, no longer pink and crumbly. Strain and get rid of extra grease. Mix in the spinach and cook for about 1 to 2 minutes until wilted. Take skillet off heat and let it cool for 10 minutes. Put the beef mixture in a bowl. Add in the pepper, garlic salt, egg, olive oil, bread crumbs, parsley and Parmesan and combine

100. Mediterranean Meatballs With Couscous

"It's quick, easy but tasty!"
Serving: 8 | Prep: 20m | Ready in: 45m

Ingredients

- Meatballs:
- cooking spray
- 1 lb. ground beef
- 1/2 cup bread crumbs
- 1 egg
- 3 tbsps. chopped fresh mint
- 2 tbsps. Greek yogurt
- 1/2 tsp. salt
- 1/2 tsp. garlic powder
- 1/2 tsp. ground cumin
- 1/4 tsp. ground black pepper
- Sauce:
- 1 tbsp. canola oil
- 1/4 onion, sliced
- 2 tbsps. all-purpose flour
- 1 (14.5 oz.) can beef broth
- 1/4 cup Greek yogurt
- 2 tbsps. chopped fresh mint
- 3 cups cooked couscous

Direction

- Start preheating oven to 350°F (175°C). Line aluminum foil on baking sheet, then spray cooking spray over.
- In a large bowl, combine pepper, cumin, garlic powder, salt, 2 tbsps. of the Greek yogurt, 3 tbsps. of mint, egg, breadcrumbs and beef. Shape into 24 meatballs. Arrange on prepared baking sheet.
- Bake in preheated oven for about 20 mins until the meatballs are no longer pink in middle.
- In a large skillet, heat oil over medium-high heat. Cook onion for about 3 mins until translucent. Put in the flour. Gradually pour in beef broth. Cook for about 2 mins until the sauce begins to thicken. Put in meatballs. Whisk in 2 tbsps. of mint and quarter cup of Greek yogurt. Add over couscous to serve.

Nutrition Information

- Calories: 258 calories;
- Total Carbohydrate: 21.4 g
- Cholesterol: 61 mg
- Total Fat: 12.1 g
- Protein: 14.8 g
- Sodium: 411 mg

101. Mediterranean Pasta With Greens

"Tasty and satisfying."
Serving: 8 | Prep: 15m | Ready in: 35m

Ingredients

- 1 (16 oz.) package dry fusilli pasta
- 1 bunch Swiss chard, stems removed
- 2 tbsps. olive oil
- 1/2 cup oil-packed sun-dried tomatoes, chopped
- 1/2 cup pitted, chopped kalamata olives
- 1/2 cup pitted, chopped green olives
- 1 clove garlic, minced
- 1/4 cup fresh grated Parmesan cheese

Direction

- Boil the lightly salted water in a large pot. Stir in the pasta, then cook until al dente for 10-12 mins. Drain.
- Put chard into a microwave safe bowl. Fill water into a bowl, about half full. Cook in the microwave on High until limp, for 5 mins; drain.
- In a skillet, heat oil over medium heat. Stir in garlic, green olives, kalamata olives and sun-dried tomatoes. Mix in chard. Cook while stirring until tender. Toss with the pasta. Top with a sprinkle of Parmesan cheese. Enjoy.

Nutrition Information

- Calories: 296 calories;
- Total Carbohydrate: 44.6 g
- Cholesterol: 2 mg
- Total Fat: 9.7 g
- Protein: 9.6 g
- Sodium: 467 mg

102. Mushroom And Sausage Rice Pilaf

"Make this wonderful rice pilaf using your preferred smoked sausage and a few more ingredients. You can also add more mushrooms if you wish."
Serving: 6 | Prep: 15m | Ready in: 1h13m

Ingredients

- 1/2 cup orzo pasta
- 1/4 cup butter, divided
- 1/2 cup chopped onion
- 3 cloves garlic, minced
- 2 cups sliced mushrooms
- 1 cup long grain white rice
- 1/2 cup chopped smoked sausage, or more to taste
- 3 1/2 cups chicken broth

Direction

- Preheat the oven to 175°C or 350°F.

- Toast the orzo pasta in an ovenproof pan on medium heat for around 5 minutes, until light brown; move to a plate.
- In the same pan, melt 2 tbsp. butter. Cook the garlic and onion for around 5 minutes, until the onion is a bit translucent. Add mushrooms and let it cook for about 5 minutes more until tender. Combine with the orzo pasta.
- Cook the white rice for about 5 minutes in the remaining 2 tbsp. butter, until the rice turns light brown. Mix in sausage, then cook for 3 minutes. Stir in mushroom mixture and cooked orzo pasta; pour in chicken broth, then boil. Take off from heat. Use an oven-proof lid to cover the pan.
- Bake for half an hour in the preheated oven, until the liquid is absorbed; stir thoroughly.

Nutrition Information

- Calories: 290 calories;
- Total Carbohydrate: 40.7 g
- Cholesterol: 30 mg
- Total Fat: 10.6 g
- Protein: 7.5 g
- Sodium: 857 mg

103. Mushroom Garlic Angel Hair Pasta

"An easy, quick and yummy dish."
Serving: 6 | Prep: 15m | Ready in: 30m

Ingredients

- 1 (8 oz.) package angel hair pasta
- 1/4 cup butter
- 3 tbsps. all-purpose flour
- 3/4 cup milk
- 2 cloves garlic, minced
- 2 tbsps. grated Parmesan cheese
- 2 tbsps. grated Asiago cheese
- 1 tbsp. extra-virgin olive oil
- 1/4 cup mushrooms, halved and sliced
- 2 tbsps. finely chopped red bell pepper
- 1/4 cup chopped green onion

- 2 tbsps. grated Parmesan cheese

Direction

- In a big pot, let lightly salted water boil. In boiling water, cook angel hair for 4 to 5 minutes until cooked through but firm to bite, stirring occasionally. Let it drain.
- Over medium heat, heat butter in a small saucepan. Into the melted butter, stir flour until well mixed, then, cook for about 3 minutes. Pour milk into flour mixture slowly, stirring constantly until well incorporated. Put garlic, cooking and stirring for about 2 minutes until sauce is thickened. Put Asiago cheese and 2 tbsps. of Parmesan cheese. Keep stirring for 2 to 4 minute until cheese is melted. Turn heat to low. While preparing remaining ingredients, simmer garlic sauce.
- Over medium-high heat, heat olive oil in a skillet. Put red bell pepper and mushrooms. Cover, then cook for about 5 minutes, until vegetables are tender, stirring occasionally. Move it away from heat.
- In a serving bowl, put angel hair pasta in. Coat it with garlic sauce by tossing. Put green onion and mushroom mixture. Gently toss. Put 2 tbsps. of Parmesan cheese on top.

Nutrition Information

- Calories: 251 calories;
- Total Carbohydrate: 26.2 g
- Cholesterol: 28 mg
- Total Fat: 13.2 g
- Protein: 7.6 g
- Sodium: 223 mg

104. My Own Mickmack

"Turn the leftovers to a tasty meal!"
Serving: 8 | Prep: 10m | Ready in: 1h10m

Ingredients

- 1 cup leftover cooked pinto beans
- 1 cup leftover cooked macaroni

- 1 cup leftover ground sausage
- 1 large onion, chopped and sauteed
- 1 (14.5 oz.) can diced tomatoes
- 1 tsp. chopped fresh parsley
- 1 tsp. ground cayenne pepper
- 1 tbsp. chopped garlic
- salt and pepper to taste

Direction

- Start preheating the oven to 350°F (175°C).
- Combine pepper, salt, garlic, cayenne pepper, parsley, tomatoes, onion, sausage, macaroni and beans in a large bowl. Mix well. Spread mixture into a lightly greased baking dish (9x13 inches).
- Bake for 60 mins at 350°F (175°C).

Nutrition Information

- Calories: 169 calories;
- Total Carbohydrate: 12 g
- Cholesterol: 20 mg
- Total Fat: 10.5 g
- Protein: 6.5 g
- Sodium: 331 mg

105. Naunie's Pastera (leftover Easter Pasta Bake)

""*Wondering what to do with the little amounts of leftover dry pasta that are in your cupboard? I use them in this Italian baked pasta recipe!*""
Serving: 24 | Prep: 30m | Ready in: 3h10m

Ingredients

- 2 1/2 tbsps. olive oil, divided
- 1/4 lb. elbow macaroni
- 1/4 lb. ziti pasta
- 1/4 lb. farfalle (bow tie) pasta
- 1/4 lb. radiatore pasta
- 1 lb. sweet Italian sausage links, cut into 1/2-inch slices
- 12 jumbo eggs, or more if needed
- 1/2 cup shredded Pecorino Romano cheese, or more if needed
- salt to taste
- 1/4 tsp. freshly ground black pepper, or more to taste
- 2 tbsps. olive oil, divided

Direction

- Prepare the oven by preheating to 350°F (175°C). Use aluminum foil to line a large baking sheet. Prepare a 2-qt. and a 1 1/2-qt. round glass baking dish then grease each with 3/4 tsp. olive oil; sprinkle 1 tbsp. of leftover olive oil into the bottom of each baking dish.
- Place a lightly salted water in a large pot and make it boil. Add radiatore pasta, farfalle, ziti and macaroni in the boiling water, and cook for 8-10 minutes, whisking occasionally, until cooked through yet firm to chew. Strain.
- Pile slices of sausage on a baking sheet lined with foil.
- Place in the preheated oven and bake for 30-45 minutes until crisp and brow in color. Minimize oven heat to 325°F (165°C).
- In a large bowl, whisk eggs with an electric mixer until foamy. Mix in the black pepper, salt, and Pecorino-Romano cheese; keep on whisking egg mixture for 2 to 3 minutes with electric mixer on highest speed until cheese and eggs are combined. Add cooked pasta into eggs and cheese; the mixture should be runny and pasta will look like floating in egg mixture. Add Pecorino-Romano cheese and additional beaten eggs into the mixture if more egg mixture is necessary. Put spoonfuls of egg-pasta mixture into each casserole, next by a layer of sausage; keep on layering pasta mixture and sausage until all sausage has been applied. Place final layer of pasta mixture on top. Sprinkle with 1 tbsp. olive oil each top of casserole. Small portions of pasta should stick out of the egg mixture.
- Place in the preheated oven and bake for about 1 hour until casseroles are set in the middle; increase oven heat to 350°F (175°C) and keep on baking for 1 to 1 1/2 more hours until the

tops of casseroles are crispy and turned brown in color.

Nutrition Information

- Calories: 192 calories;
- Total Carbohydrate: 14.9 g
- Cholesterol: 131 mg
- Total Fat: 10.4 g
- Protein: 9.9 g
- Sodium: 234 mg

106. Nic's Easiest, Creamiest Macaroni And Cheese

"This recipe with mac and cheese along with an amazing twist."
Serving: 4 | Prep: 2m | Ready in: 10m

Ingredients

- 1 (7.25 oz.) package macaroni and cheese
- 1 (10.75 oz.) can condensed cream of chicken soup

Direction

- Boil a big pot of slightly salted water. Put in pasta and cook till al dente for 8 - 10 minutes. Drain off and bring back to the pot.
- Mix condensed soup, powdered cheese mixture with pasta. Stir till coated equally.

Nutrition Information

- Calories: 256 calories;
- Total Carbohydrate: 39.9 g
- Cholesterol: 13 mg
- Total Fat: 6.3 g
- Protein: 10 g
- Sodium: 906 mg

107. Noodles And Eggs

""A recipe that is my most comfort food, thanks to years of loving it as a kid. Super pleasing while the tastes aren't sophisticated. This primary dish is practically fail-proof and is a fine way to use up leftover pasta as a side or can be an instant meal in a pinch. It was paired with ketchup in our home, but feel free to mix it up with your desired vegetables for a healthy variation.""
Serving: 4 | Prep: 10m | Ready in: 25m

Ingredients

- 1 1/2 cups elbow macaroni
- 1 tbsp. butter
- 1/4 tsp. paprika (optional)
- salt and ground black pepper to taste
- 4 large eggs, lightly beaten

Direction

- Place lightly salted water in a big pot and make it boil. Put in elbow macaroni in the simmering water and cook for 8 minutes, stirring occasionally until cooked through but firm to the bite. Drain.
- In a skillet on medium heat, put butter and melt. Place the cooked pasta on butter, without mixing. Add pepper, salt and paprika to season the pasta.
- Put the eggs on pasta and cook for 2 minutes, without stirring until eggs start to set. Stir and cook eggs and pasta for 2 minutes until eggs are almost set. Then cover skillet and separate from heat; let it sit for about 2 to 5 minutes until eggs have set.

Nutrition Information

- Calories: 243 calories;
- Total Carbohydrate: 29.9 g
- Cholesterol: 194 mg
- Total Fat: 8.5 g
- Protein: 11.5 g
- Sodium: 93 mg

108. Noodles Romanoff I

"This recipe will surprise you."
Serving: 6

Ingredients

- 1 (8 oz.) package wide egg noodles
- 1 (8 oz.) container cottage cheese
- 1 (8 oz.) container sour cream
- 1/4 tbsp. finely chopped onion
- 1/4 tsp. minced garlic
- 1/2 tsp. Worcestershire sauce
- 1 dash hot pepper sauce
- 1/2 tsp. salt
- 2 tbsps. shredded Cheddar cheese

Direction

- In a large pot, cook egg noodles in the boiling salted water until al dente, then drain.
- Mix salt, red pepper sauce, Worcestershire sauce, garlic, minced onion, sour cream and cottage cheese together in a large bowl. Stir in the cooked egg noodles. Transfer to a greased 2-qt casserole dish.
- Bake in a preheated 350°F (175°C) until bubbly and heated through or for 30 mins. Enjoy warm.

Nutrition Information

- Calories: 275 calories;
- Total Carbohydrate: 29.4 g
- Cholesterol: 57 mg
- Total Fat: 12.2 g
- Protein: 11.8 g
- Sodium: 399 mg

109. Noodles Romanoff III

""Yummy noodles cooked with cottage cheese and sour cream. Perfect on a cold winter night and paired with some dark bread, if wished. Put regular sour cream for best outcome.""
Serving: 6

Ingredients

- 8 oz. elbow macaroni
- 1 cup sour cream
- 1 cup cottage cheese
- 1 dash Worcestershire sauce (optional)
- 3 tbsps. minced onion
- 1 tsp. minced garlic (optional)
- 1/2 cup seasoned dry bread crumbs

Direction

- Prepare the oven by preheating to 350°F (175°C).
- Place a lightly salted water in a big pot and make it boil. Put in the pasta and cook for 8-10 minutes or until al dente then strain. Instantly stir the cottage cheese and sour cream into the pasta; stir together.
- Stir garlic, onion and Worcestershire sauce into the mixture, if preferred. Transfer mixture into a 2-qt.baking dish that is lightly greased and place bread crumbs on top. Place in the preheated oven and bake for 45 minutes.

Nutrition Information

- Calories: 297 calories;
- Total Carbohydrate: 37.6 g
- Cholesterol: 22 mg
- Total Fat: 10.8 g
- Protein: 12 g
- Sodium: 241 mg

110. Nutritious And Delicious Pasta

"A tasty and healthy pasta dish"
Serving: 6

Ingredients

- 8 oz. pasta
- 3 onions, minced
- 8 fresh mushrooms, sliced
- 1 tsp. onion powder
- 1 tsp. garlic powder
- 1 (5.5 oz.) can low-sodium, tomato-vegetable juice cocktail
- 1/2 cup port wine
- 1 tsp. dried oregano
- 1 bay leaf
- 1 tsp. arrowroot powder
- 1 cup water

Direction

- In a large pot, cook pasta with the boiling salted water until it is al dente, then drain well.
- In the meantime, sauté onions and mushrooms in half cup of water in a large saucepan. Put in basil, oregano, tomato vegetable juice, Port wine, onion powder and garlic. After first dissolving arrowroot in a bowl with half cup water, slowly put into saucepan, stirring frequently. Thickening will happen within a minute.
- Put cooked and drained pasta into large saucepan; stir. Put the lid on for 3 mins. Enjoy warm.

Nutrition Information

- Calories: 161 calories;
- Total Carbohydrate: 29.1 g
- Cholesterol: 27 mg
- Total Fat: 1 g
- Protein: 5.9 g
- Sodium: 29 mg

111. Olive And Feta Pasta

"This dish is so versatile."
Serving: 4 | Prep: 15m | Ready in: 35m

Ingredients

- 8 oz. uncooked whole wheat spaghetti
- 1 tbsp. olive oil
- 2 cloves garlic, minced
- 8 oz. crimini mushrooms, sliced
- 2 small zucchini, sliced
- dried oregano to taste
- salt and pepper to taste
- 12 black olives, pitted and sliced
- 1 oz. crumbled feta cheese

Direction

- Boil the lightly salted water in a large pot. Put in spaghetti. Cook until al dente or 8-10 mins; drain.
- In a skillet, heat olive oil over medium heat. Sauté garlic for 2 mins. Mix in zucchini and mushrooms. Season with pepper, salt, and oregano. Stir in the olives. Cook until heated through. In the skillet, put pasta; coat by tossing. Keep cooking for about 2 mins. Add feta cheese on top. Enjoy.

Nutrition Information

- Calories: 274 calories;
- Total Carbohydrate: 43.5 g
- Cholesterol: 6 mg
- Total Fat: 7.4 g
- Protein: 12.1 g
- Sodium: 242 mg

112. One Pot Pasta

"This one is sure to become your family favorite!"
Serving: 4

Ingredients

- 1 tsp. olive oil

- 1/2 cup sliced onion
- 1 cup fresh sliced mushrooms
- 1 (29 oz.) can diced tomatoes
- 1 (8 oz.) can tomato sauce
- 1 cup water
- 2 tsps. dried basil
- 1 tsp. dried oregano
- 1 tsp. white sugar
- 1/4 tsp. garlic powder
- 1/4 tsp. ground black pepper
- 8 oz. macaroni

Direction

- Spray nonstick cooking spray over a large nonstick pan. Put in oil, heat over medium flame. Put in mushrooms and onion. Cook until tender, stirring frequently, for 3-5 mins.
- Put spices, sugar, water, tomato sauce and tomatoes into skillet. Stir in pasta once the mixture starts to boil. Lower the heat to medium-low, cover and cook for 20 mins. While cooking, stir mixture every 4-5 mins.

Nutrition Information

- Calories: 290 calories;
- Total Carbohydrate: 55.2 g
- Cholesterol: 0 mg
- Total Fat: 2.3 g
- Protein: 10.6 g
- Sodium: 775 mg

113.One-pot Spinach Mushroom Lasagna

""Enjoy this rich and creamy lasagna dish that's so tasty, you wouldn't believe it's a one-pan dish!""
Serving: 12

Ingredients

- 1 tbsp. olive oil
- 8 oz. baby bella (crimini) mushrooms, chopped
- 1 tsp. crushed red pepper flakes, or to taste

- 5 oz. fresh baby spinach, chopped
- 1 (24 oz.) jar Ragu® Old World Style® Traditional Sauce
- 3 cups water
- 12 uncooked lasagna noodles, broken into 2-inch pieces
- 1 1/4 cups part-skim ricotta cheese
- 3/4 cup shredded part-skim mozzarella cheese
- Grated Parmesan cheese for garnish (optional)

Direction

- Set a big saucepan on medium-high heat, and heat up some oil. Cook the mushrooms in the oil for 5 minutes or until they become soft. Mix in spinach and red pepper flakes; cook until the spinach is wilted. Mix water and a meat-based sauce; boil. Mix in the uncooked noodles. Lower the heat to medium and cover. Let the noodles cook for 20 minutes or until the noodles are tender. Make sure to stir frequently to avoid having the noodles stick on the bottom.
- Place spoonfuls of ricotta cheese on top of the noodles then add a sprinkling of mozzarella cheese. Lower the heat and allow to simmer while covered for 5 minutes or until the cheese has melted. Garnish with grated Parmesan cheese.

Nutrition Information

- Calories: 196 calories;
- Total Carbohydrate: 25.6 g
- Cholesterol: 13 mg
- Total Fat: 6.1 g
- Protein: 9.9 g
- Sodium: 441 mg

114. One-pot Vegetarian Chili Mac

"Your family will enjoy this delicious dish!"
Serving: 6 | Prep: 5m | Ready in: 20m

Ingredients

- 1 box Barilla® Pronto™ Cut-Macaroni

- 3 cups low sodium vegetable broth (or water)
- 2 cloves garlic, minced
- 1/2 cup onion, chopped
- 1 bell pepper, chopped
- 1 (15 oz.) can beans of choice, drained & rinsed (kidney, white, black and blends all work great for this!)
- 1 (14.5 oz.) can diced tomatoes
- 1 1/2 tbsps. chili powder
- 1 tsp. cumin
- 1 (10 oz.) bag spinach
- 4 oz. sharp Cheddar cheese
- Fresh parsley
- Salt and pepper to taste

Direction

- In the pot, put spices, tomatoes, beans, bell pepper, onions, garlic and Barilla(R) Pronto(TM) pasta.
- POUR IN water/broth. Cook over the high heat.
- PUT IN the spinach after 5 mins.
- Keep cooking for 5 to 10 mins, stirring occasionally, until spinach has wilted, and all the liquid has absorbed.
- While chili mac is warm, mix in cheese.
- Add fresh parsley on top. Enjoy!

Nutrition Information

- Calories: 190 calories;
- Total Carbohydrate: 21.4 g
- Cholesterol: 20 mg
- Total Fat: 7.2 g
- Protein: 11.2 g
- Sodium: 563 mg

115. Onion Elk Roast Stroganoff

"It's the super yummy and super easy recipe."
Serving: 6 | Prep: 15m | Ready in: 5h45m

Ingredients

- 1 1/2 lbs. elk roast

- 1 1/2 tbsps. steak seasoning
- 1 tsp. rubbed sage
- 1 small onion, chopped
- 4 cloves garlic, chopped
- 1 (10.75 oz.) can cream of onion soup
- 1 cup water
- 1 cup sour cream

Direction

- Season sage and steak seasoning to elk roast. Put into the slow cooker along with water, cream of onion soup, garlic and onion. Cook, covered, on Low for 5-7 hours until elk is shredded with fork easily. Stir in sour cream. Cook for half an hour more. Shred meat, then serve.

Nutrition Information

- Calories: 242 calories;
- Total Carbohydrate: 9.5 g
- Cholesterol: 75 mg
- Total Fat: 11.6 g
- Protein: 24.1 g
- Sodium: 1140 mg

116. Orzo And Chicken Stuffed Peppers

"A tasty and beautiful dish with red, yellow, and green peppers. You can use Smart Balance® spread and chicken broth with low sodium for this dish."
Serving: 6 | Prep: 20m | Ready in: 55m

Ingredients

- cooking spray
- 1 green bell pepper - halved, seeded, and stem removed
- 1 red bell pepper - halved, seeded, and stem removed
- 1 yellow bell pepper - halved, seeded, and stem removed
- 1 tbsp. butter
- 2 tbsps. olive oil

- 3 green onions, sliced
- 4 cloves garlic, minced
- 2 skinless, boneless chicken breast halves, cut into 1/2-inch cubes
- 1 tsp. ground black pepper
- 1 tsp. ground cumin
- 1 cup orzo
- 1 (16 oz.) can chicken broth
- 3 tbsps. Parmesan cheese
- 1 tsp. olive oil
- 1 tsp. butter
- 2 portobello mushrooms, thinly sliced
- 1 green onion, thinly sliced
- salt and ground black pepper to taste

Direction

- Preheat the oven to 190°C or 375°F.
- Using cooking spray, spritz the insides of the yellow, red and green bell pepper halves; arrange on a baking sheet.
- Bake the peppers for about 10 minutes in the preheated oven, until it turns a bit tender.
- Heat the 2 tbsp. oil and 1 tbsp. butter in a pan on medium heat. Cook and stir the garlic and onion for 2-3 minutes, until aromatic. Add cumin, black pepper and chicken and let it cook for 4-5 minutes, until the juices run clear and the middle of the chicken is not pink. Add chicken broth and orzo and let it simmer for around 11 minutes, until the broth is absorbed, and the orzo is completely cooked yet firm to chew. Scoop the orzo-chicken mixture into the bell peppers, then sprinkle Parmesan cheese on top.
- Bake for around 7 minutes in the preheated oven, until the cheese melts.
- Heat 1 tsp each of butter and oil in a pan. Cook and stir the leftover green onion and portobello mushrooms for around 5 minutes, until tender. Sprinkle black pepper and salt to season. Scoop approximately 2 tbsp. of mushroom mixture on each stuffed bell pepper.

Nutrition Information

- Calories: 294 calories;

- Total Carbohydrate: 33.2 g
- Cholesterol: 33 mg
- Total Fat: 10.8 g
- Protein: 16 g
- Sodium: 476 mg

117. Pad Kee Mao

"Many vendors in Bangkok made this "drunken" stir-fry."
Serving: 4 | Prep: 20m | Ready in: 1h40m

Ingredients

- 3 1/2 oz. dried Thai-style rice noodles, wide (such as Chantaboon Rice Noodles)
- 1 1/2 tsps. olive oil
- 2 cloves garlic, minced
- 1/2 tsp. thick soy sauce
- 2 tsps. white sugar
- 1 1/2 tsps. olive oil
- 2 cloves garlic, minced
- 1/2 lb. pork (any cut), thinly sliced
- 1 serrano pepper, minced, or more to taste
- 30 fresh basil leaves, chopped
- 1/2 tsp. thick soy sauce
- 1 tsp. white sugar
- 1 tsp. salt
- 1/2 cup bean sprouts

Direction

- Put dry rice noodles inside a bowl. Cover using hot water and soak for about an hour until soft and white. Drain noodles then put aside.
- In a big skillet or wok, heat 1 1/2 tsp. of olive oil on low heat. Sauté 2 minced garlic cloves for 2-3 minutes until it starts to crisp and brown in color. Mix in 2 tsps. of sugar, 1/2 tsp. of thick soy sauce, and soaked noodles until noodles absorb soy sauce and become brown in color for about 3 minutes. Take noodles out of skillet.
- Heat leftover 1 1/2 tsps. of olive oil in a wok on low heat. Mix in leftover 2 minced garlic cloves then cook for 2-3 minutes until it starts

to brown and crisp. Bring heat up to medium-high and mix in salt, 1 tsp. of sugar, 1/2 tsp. of thick soy sauce, basil, serrano pepper, and pork. Sauté for about 5 minutes until pork isn't pink and the meat edges are starting to brown. Put noodles back in wok and mix in bean sprouts. Sauté for about 5 more minutes until heated through.

Nutrition Information

- Calories: 218 calories;
- Total Carbohydrate: 26.2 g
- Cholesterol: 22 mg
- Total Fat: 9.1 g
- Protein: 7.2 g
- Sodium: 707 mg

118. Paleo Spaghetti Pie (grain, Gluten, And Dairy Free)

"An incredibly good paleo recipe."
Serving: 6 | Prep: 15m | Ready in: 1h45m

Ingredients

- 1 large spaghetti squash, halved lengthwise and seeded
- 1 lb. ground turkey sausage
- 1/2 cup diced onion
- 1 cup pizza sauce
- 1 cup coarsely chopped baby spinach leaves
- 1/2 cup diced red bell pepper
- 1/4 cup unsweetened applesauce
- 1 tsp. dried basil
- 1/2 tsp. garlic powder
- 1/2 tsp. dried oregano
- 1/4 tsp. ground black pepper
- 3 eggs, beaten

Direction

- Preheat an oven to 200 °C or 400 °F. On a baking sheet, set spaghetti squash cut-side facing down.

- In the prepped oven, allow the squash to bake for 25 minutes till cooked completely. Once cool enough to touch, using a spoon, scrape out squash strands and put in a square 8-inch baking dish.
- Lower oven temperature to 175 °C or 350 °F.
- In a big skillet over medium-high heat, let cook and mix onion and turkey sausage for 4 to 6 minutes till turkey is browned. Take off from heat and into the turkey mixture, mix black pepper, oregano, garlic powder, basil, applesauce, red bell pepper, spinach and pizza sauce. In baking dish, scatter mixture on top of squash.
- Put eggs on top of turkey mixture and combine squash, turkey mixture and egg together till egg is just incorporated.
- In the prepped oven, let bake for an hour till eggs are firm and mixture is bubbling.

Nutrition Information

- Calories: 295 calories;
- Total Carbohydrate: 29.8 g
- Cholesterol: 152 mg
- Total Fat: 13 g
- Protein: 19.2 g
- Sodium: 775 mg

119. Pan-fried Chinese Dumplings

""These little dumplings or potstickers are quick and easy to cook and taste great when served with soy sauce or your preferred Chinese dipping sauce.""
Serving: 8 | Prep: 30m | Ready in: 1h37m

Ingredients

- 2 tbsps. small dried prawns
- 1/4 cup rice vermicelli
- 3 eggs
- 1 pinch salt
- 1 tbsp. vegetable oil
- 2 bunches Chinese chives, finely chopped
- 2 mushrooms, finely chopped
- 1 tbsp. vegetable oil

- 1/2 tsp. salt
- 1/4 tsp. sesame oil
- 1 pinch ground black pepper
- 40 round wonton wrappers
- 1 1/4 cups boiling water
- 1 tbsp. vegetable oil, or as needed

Direction

- Place the dried prawns in a bowl of hot water and soak for half an hour. Drain the prawns and chop them finely.
- Place the rice vermicelli in a bowl of warm water and soak for 10 minutes. Let it drain, squeezing out any excess water, and chop finely.
- Whisk eggs in a bowl and add 1 pinch of salt. Whisk them thoroughly until foamy and light. Place the wok or large skillet over medium heat, and heat 1 tbsp. of oil. Cook the eggs for 2 minutes until set. Turn the omelet over and cook for 1 minute extra. Let cool on a clean work surface and cut into small pieces.
- Combine 1 tbsp. of oil, 1/2 tsp. of salt, mushrooms, sesame oil, chives, black pepper, egg, vermicelli, and prawns in a large bowl.
- Moisten the edge of a wonton wrapper with water. Spoon 1 tbsp. of the egg mixture into the center of the wrapper and fold it in half. Use your fingers to pleat the edges of the wrapper. Do the same with the remaining egg mixture and wrappers.
- Heat 1 tbsp. of oil in a large skillet over medium-high heat and cook half of the dumplings for 2 minutes. Stir in boiling water and cover the skillet. Bring to simmer for 10 minutes until the bottoms of the dumplings are golden brown. Remove from heat and cook the remaining dumplings.

Nutrition Information

- Calories: 217 calories;
- Total Carbohydrate: 28 g
- Cholesterol: 76 mg
- Total Fat: 8 g
- Protein: 8.3 g
- Sodium: 425 mg

120. Party Pancit

""*A typical Pinoy recipe that's even better the next morning!*""

Serving: 8 | Prep: 15m | Ready in: 30m

Ingredients

- 1/2 tbsp. sesame oil
- 2 cloves garlic, minced
- 2 tsps. minced fresh ginger root
- 1 bunch green onions, chopped into 1 inch pieces
- 2 hot chile peppers, minced
- 1 (8 oz.) package fresh mushrooms, sliced
- 1 cup chopped cooked chicken breast
- 1 cup peeled, chopped shrimp
- 3 links spicy pork sausage, sliced
- 1/2 cup sake
- 1/4 cup soy sauce
- 7 cups chicken broth
- 1 (12 oz.) package rice noodles
- 1/2 lb. fresh bean sprouts
- 1/2 lb. snow peas

Direction

- Sauté sausage, shrimp, chicken, mushrooms, chile peppers, green onion, ginger, and garlic in the hot oil in a large Dutch oven or wok until the sausage is lightly browned and shrimp turns pink. Mix in the soy sauce and sake and simmer for 2-3 minutes. Cover and reserve.
- Add chicken broth in a large saucepan then make it to a rolling boil. Put in the noodles then cook for 2 minutes over high heat. Drain instantly and rinse with cold water.
- Put the shrimp mixture over medium heat and put the bean sprouts; stir-fry for 2 minutes. Mix in the snow pear and stir-fry for 2 minutes. Mix in noodles and toss until well combined. Serve right away.

Nutrition Information

- Calories: 261 calories;
- Total Carbohydrate: 35.9 g
- Cholesterol: 41 mg
- Total Fat: 5.2 g
- Protein: 13.6 g
- Sodium: 568 mg

121.Passover Matzo Lasagna

"Let's enjoy a great meal!"
Serving: 12 | Prep: 20m | Ready in: 50m

Ingredients

- 6 matzo sheets
- 4 eggs, lightly beaten
- 1 (24 oz.) carton cottage cheese
- 1 (8 oz.) package shredded mozzarella cheese, divided
- 1 (28 oz.) jar marinara sauce

Direction

- Start preheating oven to 350°F (175°C).
- In a large bowl, soak the matzo sheets in hot water for about half a minute until tender. Drain. In a bowl, combine half mozzarella cheese, cottage cheese and eggs. Pour 1/2 cup of the marinara sauce onto bottom of a baking pan (9x13 inches). Arrange two matzo sheets over sauce. Pour over sheets with another sauce layer. Spread the top with half cheese mixture, then another sauce layer. Continue the layering until all matzo sheets are used, finishing with a sauce layer. Sprinkle top with remaining mozzarella cheese.
- Bake in preheated oven for 30-40 mins until sauce is bubbly and cheese melts.

Nutrition Information

- Calories: 242 calories;
- Total Carbohydrate: 23.2 g
- Cholesterol: 84 mg
- Total Fat: 8.9 g

- Protein: 16.4 g
- Sodium: 637 mg

---

122. Pasta Ai Fiori Di Zucca (pasta With Zucchini Blossoms)

"The flavor of this dish is so amazing."
Serving: 4 | Prep: 15m | Ready in: 45m

Ingredients

- 1/2 tsp. salt
- 1 (8 oz.) package penne pasta
- 15 fresh zucchini blossoms
- 2 tbsps. extra-virgin olive oil
- 3 cloves garlic, minced
- 1 bunch fresh parsley, chopped
- 1 tsp. saffron threads
- 2 tbsps. fine cornmeal
- 2 tbsps. grated Parmesan cheese
- salt and freshly ground black pepper to taste

Direction

- Fill water into large pot, mix in half tsp. of salt. Boil. Mix in the penne. Bring back to a boil. Cook the pasta, uncovered, for about 11 mins until the pasta has cooked through yet firm to the bite, stirring occasionally, then drain, saving half cup of pasta-cooking water.
- Clean and rinse the zucchini blossoms, discarding inner parts (anthers or stigma); chop flowers coarsely.
- In a large skillet, heat the olive oil over medium-low heat. In hot oil, cook while stirring garlic for 3-5 mins until it starts to brown. Stir the reserved half cup of pasta-cooking water, saffron, and parsley into skillet; combine by stirring. Put in zucchini blossoms. Simmer for about 10 mins until tender. Sprinkle the cornmeal over the mixture, then constantly stir for about 5 mins until thickened.
- Fold the penne pasta gently into the zucchini blossom mixture. Add black pepper, salt and Parmesan cheese on top.

Nutrition Information

- Calories: 299 calories;
- Total Carbohydrate: 46.4 g
- Cholesterol: 2 mg
- Total Fat: 9 g
- Protein: 9.4 g
- Sodium: 342 mg

123. Pasta And Beans

"A quick Italian recipe."
Serving: 4 | Prep: 10m | Ready in: 20m

Ingredients

- 1 1/2 tbsps. extra virgin olive oil
- 1 onion, chopped
- 2 tomatoes, chopped
- 1 (15 oz.) can cannellini beans
- 2 cups penne pasta
- salt to taste

Direction

- Heat olive oil in a medium-sized saucepan. Sauté onion till tender. Mix entire can of beans and tomatoes in. simmer it for 10 minutes.
- Boil a big pot with lightly salted water. Put penne pasta. Cook till al dente for 8-10 minutes; drain.
- Stir pasta with salt as desired and bean mixture.

Nutrition Information

- Calories: 279 calories;
- Total Carbohydrate: 46 g
- Cholesterol: 0 mg
- Total Fat: 6.4 g
- Protein: 9.8 g
- Sodium: 228 mg

124. Pasta And Veggies In Coconut Oil

""A spin on pasta tossed in olive oil. It's simple, fast, and nutritious meal that even children will eat without a hassle. It's truly yummy; you can put any spiced and herbs that fit your taste. This is my kid's well-loved dish, and I have to agree, I enjoy it also!""
Serving: 6 | Prep: 10m | Ready in: 24m

Ingredients

- 1 (12 oz.) package elbow macaroni
- 2 cups frozen mixed vegetables
- 1 tbsp. coconut oil, or more to taste
- 1 pinch garlic powder
- sea salt and freshly ground black pepper to taste
- 1 tbsp. grated Parmesan cheese, or to taste

Direction

- Boil lightly salted water in a big pot. Put in elbow macaroni and cook for 3 minutes, stirring occasionally, until slightly soft. Place in frozen vegetables; stir and cook for 5 minutes until tender but firm to chew. Strain in a bowl.
- In the warm pot, put coconut oil. Stir in the pepper, sea salt, garlic powder and macaroni mixture; then toss for 1 to 2 minutes until blended. Place Parmesan cheese on top.

Nutrition Information

- Calories: 266 calories;
- Total Carbohydrate: 49.3 g
- Cholesterol: < 1 mg
- Total Fat: 3.6 g
- Protein: 9.5 g
- Sodium: 68 mg

125. Pasta Chicken And Sun-dried Tomatoes

"Easy, quick, delicious and healthy!"
Serving: 8

Ingredients

- 1 (8 oz.) package tri-colored farfalle (bow tie) pasta
- 4 skinless, boneless chicken breast halves
- 1/4 cup olive oil
- 1/2 cup sun-dried tomatoes
- 1 zucchini, steamed and cut into chunks
- 1 summer squash, steamed and chopped

Direction

- In large pot with salted boiling water, put pasta. Allow to cook until al dente or for 8-10 mins, then drain.
- In the meantime, in a medium pan, sauté the chicken breasts over medium high heat. Sauté until juices run clear and chicken has cooked through or 8-10 mins per side. Take the chicken out from the skillet. Slice into bite size pieces.
- Coat the cooked pasta in large mixing bowl with oil by tossing. Put in squash, zucchini, sun-dried tomatoes and chicken pieces. Toss again. Lastly, put in cheese. Enjoy.

Nutrition Information

- Calories: 241 calories;
- Total Carbohydrate: 23.9 g
- Cholesterol: 34 mg
- Total Fat: 8.3 g
- Protein: 18.4 g
- Sodium: 114 mg

126. Pasta Melanzana

"Great flavor."
Serving: 4 | Prep: 10m | Ready in: 25m

Ingredients

- 3/4 cup bow tie (farfalle) pasta
- 1 medium eggplant, peeled and cubed
- 4 tbsps. olive oil
- 4 cloves garlic, finely chopped
- 1 tbsp. butter
- 3 cups fresh spinach, chopped
- 3 tbsps. fresh lemon juice
- salt and pepper
- 3/4 cup grated Parmesan cheese, divided
- cracked black pepper to taste

Direction

- Boil the lightly salted water in a large pot. Put in pasta. Cook until al dente or 8 to 10 mins, then drain. Keep it warm.
- In the meantime, in a skillet, heat butter and olive oil over medium heat. Put in garlic and cook while stirring until softened. Stir in eggplant. Allow eggplant to cook without stirring for 5 mins. Cook while stirring for about 5 mins more until tender.
- Mix in spinach. Add pepper and salt to season. Cook for 3 mins, stirring occasionally. Stir in lemon juice and drained pasta along with half cup of the Parmesan cheese. Move to the serving dish. Add cracked black pepper and remaining cheese on top.

Nutrition Information

- Calories: 297 calories;
- Total Carbohydrate: 16.6 g
- Cholesterol: 24 mg
- Total Fat: 22.3 g
- Protein: 10.5 g
- Sodium: 329 mg

127. Pasta Primavera With Cauliflower Sauce

"It's sure to become one of your favorites!"
Serving: 4 | Prep: 15m | Ready in: 40m

Ingredients

- 1 tbsp. olive oil
- 1/2 cup chopped onion
- 2 cloves garlic, minced
- 3 cups cauliflower florets
- 3/4 cup vegetable broth
- 1/2 cup finely shredded Parmesan cheese, plus more for garnish
- 1/3 cup water
- 1/8 tsp. black pepper
- 6 oz. multigrain spaghetti, uncooked
- 4 cups broccoli florets, cut into 1-inch pieces
- 1 red bell pepper, cut into bite-size strips
- 2 tbsps. sliced fresh basil
- 1 tsp. lemon zest (optional)
- 1 tbsp. lemon juice

Direction

- In a small saucepan, heat oil over medium heat. Put in garlic and onion. Cook for 3-4 mins until onion is tender, stirring occasionally. Stir in broth and cauliflower. Boil. Lower the heat. Cover and simmer for about 15 mins until tender. Uncover; allow to cool slightly. Place into a food processor. Put in black pepper, water and cheese. Pulse, covered, until they become smooth.
- In the meantime, cook pasta following the package instructions. In the last 5 mins, put in bell pepper and broccoli. Drain, saving half cup of cooking water.
- Put the pasta mixture back to pot. Mix in the cauliflower sauce. Heat through; if needed, stir in the reserved cooking water to reach preferred consistency. Decorate with more cheese, basil, lemon juice and zest, if using.

Nutrition Information

- Calories: 295 calories;
- Total Carbohydrate: 47.7 g
- Cholesterol: 7 mg
- Total Fat: 7.3 g
- Protein: 14.9 g
- Sodium: 314 mg

128. Pasta Strega Nonna

"Fast and simple Italian inspired stir-fry pasta! Match it up over short pasta – orecchiette, farfalle or shells."
Serving: 4 | Prep: 10m | Ready in: 20m

Ingredients

- 3 tbsps. olive oil
- 1/2 lb. cooked and peeled shrimp
- 1 lb. fresh asparagus, trimmed and coarsely chopped
- 1 tbsp. minced garlic
- hot sauce to taste
- salt to taste
- 1 tbsp. grated Romano cheese

Direction

- In a medium-low heat, place a large skillet and heat olive oil. Add in garlic, shrimp, and asparagus. Sauté until asparagus turns bright green and slightly tender. Add in salt and hot sauce; mix. Sprinkle with Romano cheese. Ready to serve.

Nutrition Information

- Calories: 190 calories;
- Total Carbohydrate: 5 g
- Cholesterol: 117 mg
- Total Fat: 11.9 g
- Protein: 17.4 g
- Sodium: 199 mg

129. Pasta With Grilled Shrimp And Pineapple Salsa

"A citrusy and refreshing recipe with only 20 minutes preparation."
Serving: 6 | Prep: 15m | Ready in: 35m

Ingredients

- 3 cups rotini pasta
- 1/2 fresh pineapple - peeled, cored and chopped
- 1 large red bell pepper, chopped
- 1 large red onion, chopped
- 1 jalapeno pepper, seeded and minced
- 1/2 cup fresh orange juice
- 1/3 cup fresh lime juice
- 1 1/2 lbs. large shrimp - peeled and deveined

Direction

- Boil lightly salted water in a large pot. Cook pasta in boiling water until al dente, about 8 to 10 minutes. Drain well.
- Mix together lime juice, orange juice, jalapeno pepper, red onion, red pepper and pineapple in a large bowl until well combined. Set aside.
- Prepare an outdoor grill; set the oiled rack 6 inches from coals. On gas grill, set the high heat. Grill each side of the shrimp for 2 minutes.
- Stir the cooked noodles into the salsa. Place shrimp on pasta and it's ready to serve.

Nutrition Information

- Calories: 271 calories;
- Total Carbohydrate: 34.1 g
- Cholesterol: 173 mg
- Total Fat: 2.8 g
- Protein: 27.7 g
- Sodium: 172 mg

130. Pasta, Chicken And Artichokes

"Amazing flavor!"
Serving: 4 | Prep: 25m | Ready in: 40m

Ingredients

- 4 oz. uncooked pasta
- 1 tsp. olive oil
- 1 tsp. minced garlic
- 3 skinless, boneless chicken breast halves - cut into strips
- 1/4 cup chicken broth
- 1/4 cup fresh chopped broccoli
- 1/4 cup chopped tomatoes
- 1/4 (14 oz.) can artichoke hearts, drained and sliced
- 1/4 cup fresh sliced mushrooms
- 1/4 cup chopped red bell pepper
- salt and pepper to taste
- 4 tbsps. grated Parmesan cheese
- 1 tbsp. chopped fresh parsley

Direction

- Bring a large pot of water to a boil. Cook pasta in boiling water until done. Drain, and put aside.
- Heat olive oil in a large sauté pan over medium high heat. In oil, brown garlic and chicken for about 5 mins. Discard from pan. Put aside.
- In the pan, pour the chicken broth. Put in tomato and broccoli. Cook for about 5 mins. Mix in pasta, cooked chicken, red bell pepper, mushrooms and artichoke hearts. Cook until hot or for 3-5 mins longer. Season with pepper and salt to taste.
- Place into the serving bowl, add parsley and Parmesan cheese on top. Enjoy.

Nutrition Information

- Calories: 267 calories;
- Total Carbohydrate: 25.6 g
- Cholesterol: 49 mg
- Total Fat: 7.5 g

- Protein: 23.2 g
- Sodium: 267 mg

131.Pastachutta

"Your kids will very like this!"
Serving: 8 | Prep: 10m | Ready in: 30m

Ingredients

- 1 (16 oz.) package spaghetti
- 1/4 cup butter
- 4 cloves garlic, thinly sliced
- 1 (8 oz.) package fresh mushrooms, sliced
- 1 onion, chopped
- salt and pepper to taste

Direction

- Boil the lightly salted water in a large pot. Put in spaghetti. Cook until al dente or for 8-10 mins, then drain, do not rinse.
- In the meantime, in a large pan, melt butter over medium-high heat. Sauté onion, mushrooms and garlic until tender. Toss with the cooked spaghetti. Season to taste with pepper and salt.

Nutrition Information

- Calories: 272 calories;
- Total Carbohydrate: 44.7 g
- Cholesterol: 15 mg
- Total Fat: 6.7 g
- Protein: 8.1 g
- Sodium: 46 mg

132. Pea And Pancetta Ramen "risotto"

"In this recipe, an instant ramen is used instead of risotto for a quick and yummy dinner meal."
Serving: 4 | Prep: 5m | Ready in: 20m

Ingredients

- 1/2 cup diced pancetta or bacon
- 1 tbsp. olive oil
- 1 medium onion, chopped
- 1/4 tsp. salt
- 1 (3 oz.) package ramen noodles, coarsely broken in package (flavor packet discarded)
- 1 (10 oz.) package frozen peas
- 3 cups low-sodium chicken broth
- 1 tbsp. butter
- 1/2 cup grated Parmesan cheese, plus additional for serving
- 1/4 tsp. freshly ground black pepper

Direction

- Put the oil and bacon or pancetta in a 12-inch non-stick skillet and let the bacon or pancetta cook on medium heat while stirring it from time to time for 5 minutes until it is starting to turn brown in color. Put in the salt and onion and sauté it for about 4 minutes until the onion is soft. Put in the noodles and let it cook for 1 minute while stirring. Put in the broth and peas and let the mixture boil. Keep cooking the mixture for about 3 minutes until the noodles have started to soften.
- Take the skillet out from the heat and add in the Parmesan, pepper and butter. In case the mixture is still a bit runny, let it sit for 1-2 more minutes to let the noodles absorb some of the liquid. Serve it with extra Parmesan if you want.

Nutrition Information

- Calories: 297 calories;
- Total Carbohydrate: 15.4 g
- Cholesterol: 35 mg
- Total Fat: 20.4 g

- Protein: 13.2 g
- Sodium: 746 mg

133. Penne Pesto Pasta Salad

"This dish never fails to get compliments."
Serving: 8 | Prep: 10m | Ready in: 25m

Ingredients

- 1 (8 oz.) package truRoots® Ancient Grains Organic Penne
- 1/2 cup prepared fresh basil pesto
- 1 (8 oz.) container mozzarella pearls (perline)*
- 1 pint grape or cherry tomatoes, halved
- 1/4 cup grated Parmesan cheese
- 1 (2.25 oz.) can sliced black olives, drained
- Fresh basil sprigs, for garnish (optional)

Direction

- In large pot, cook pasta in the boiling salted water for about 7-9 mins until it is just al dente. Drain.
- In large bowl, combine pesto and pasta. Stir in olives, Parmesan, tomatoes and mozzarella. Let chill until ready to serv. If desired, decorate with the basil sprigs. Enjoy!

Nutrition Information

- Calories: 285 calories;
- Total Carbohydrate: 24.8 g
- Cholesterol: 29 mg
- Total Fat: 15.8 g
- Protein: 11.2 g
- Sodium: 269 mg

134. Penne With Peppers And Sausage

"It's quick, easy but tasty!"
Serving: 6 | Prep: 20m | Ready in: 54m

Ingredients

- 1 1/2 cups whole wheat penne pasta
- cooking spray
- 2 green bell peppers, cut into thin strips
- 1 onion, thinly sliced
- 1 cup fresh mushrooms, sliced
- 1 clove garlic, minced
- 1 (16 oz.) package spicy Italian turkey sausage, casings removed
- 1/4 tsp. red pepper flakes
- 1/4 tsp. salt
- 1/8 tsp. ground black pepper
- 1/8 tsp. dried oregano
- 1 (14.5 oz.) can diced tomatoes
- 1/4 cup grated Parmesan cheese
- 2 tbsps. grated Parmesan cheese

Direction

- Boil the lightly salted water in a large pot. Put in penne; cook for about 11 mins until tender but firm to bite, stirring occasionally. Drain.
- Coat cooking spray over a large nonstick frying pan; set over medium-high heat. Put in garlic, mushrooms, onion and green bell peppers. Cook for 7-8 mins until almost tender, stirring frequently.
- In a skillet, put turkey sausage over medium heat; cook while stirring for about 6 mins until crumbly and browned, breaking the sausage up using wooden spoon. Put in oregano, black pepper, salt and red pepper flakes; mix in tomatoes. Simmer for about 5 mins until heated through.
- In serving bowl, put penne. Add sausage mixture on top; add a sprinkle of Parmesan cheese over.

Nutrition Information

- Calories: 210 calories;

- Total Carbohydrate: 14.4 g
- Cholesterol: 62 mg
- Total Fat: 9.4 g
- Protein: 18.9 g
- Sodium: 901 mg

135. Pesto Pasta

"This flavorful but easy recipe can be served warm or cold."
Serving: 8 | Prep: 5m | Ready in: 15m

Ingredients

- 1/2 cup chopped onion
- 2 1/2 tbsps. pesto
- 2 tbsps. olive oil
- 2 tbsps. grated Parmesan cheese
- 1 (16 oz.) package pasta
- salt to taste
- ground black pepper to taste

Direction

- In a big pot of boiling water, cook pasta till done. Drain.
- On medium low heat, heat the oil in one frying pan at the same time. Put in pepper, salt, onion and pesto. Cook till onions turn tender for roughly 5 minutes.
- Stir pesto mixture into pasta in a big bowl. Mix in grated cheese. Serve.

Nutrition Information

- Calories: 225 calories;
- Total Carbohydrate: 32 g
- Cholesterol: 44 mg
- Total Fat: 7.2 g
- Protein: 7.8 g
- Sodium: 71 mg

136. Pierogi Dough

"It's sure to become one of your favorites!"
Serving: 30

Ingredients

- 4 cups all-purpose flour
- 1 tsp. salt
- 2 tsps. vegetable oil
- 1/4 tsp. baking powder
- 1 cup warm water
- 1 egg, beaten

Direction

- Mix baking powder, salt, and flour together in a large bowl. Create a well in middle.
- Mix beaten egg, warm water and vegetable oil together in separate bowl. Pour to well of dry ingredients. Knead the dough for 8-10 mins.
- Cover the dough and allow to rest for 120 mins. Roll out, then fill as preferred.

Nutrition Information

- Calories: 66 calories;
- Total Carbohydrate: 12.7 g
- Cholesterol: 6 mg
- Total Fat: 0.6 g
- Protein: 1.9 g
- Sodium: 84 mg

137. Pierogi From Granny

"The best treat for your family!"
Serving: 50 | Prep: 1h | Ready in: 1h45m

Ingredients

- 3 large potatoes - peeled and cubed
- 2 tbsps. butter
- 3 slices bacon, finely chopped
- 3 onions, finely chopped
- 1 1/2 lbs. ground beef
- 1/2 lb. ground pork
- 1 (8 oz.) package mushrooms, minced

- 1 tbsp. chicken bouillon granules
- salt and pepper to taste
- 1 tbsp. chopped fresh dill
- 3 2/3 cups all-purpose flour
- 1 cup self-rising flour
- 2 eggs, lightly beaten
- 1 pinch salt
- 1 cup water, or as needed
- 1 egg, beaten
- 1/4 cup butter

Direction

- In a large pot, put potatoes; add salted water to cover. Boil. Lower the heat to medium-low, simmer, covered, for about 20 mins until tender. Drain; let steam dry for 1-2 mins. Mash.
- In the meantime, in a large pot, melt 2 tbsps. of the butter over medium-high heat. Put in bacon. Cook for about 5 mins until bacon starts to brown and fat starts to render. Stir in onion. Keep cooking for about 5 mins until onion turns translucent and softens. Stir in ground pork and ground beef. Keep cooking for about 10 mins until no longer pink and crumbly. Lastly, stir in dill, pepper, salt, chicken bouillon and minced mushrooms. Cook, covered, for about 5 more mins until mushrooms soften. Stir in mashed potatoes. Put filling aside and let cool.
- In a large bowl, whisk together self-rising flour and all-purpose flour. Create a well in the middle. Pour in enough water, salt and two beaten eggs to make soft dough. On well-floured work surface, knead until they become pliable and smooth. Roll dough into 1/8-inch thickness. Slice into 5-inch circles.
- Spoon filling onto 1 side of every dough rounds. Use remaining beaten egg to moisten edges. Fold to make 1/2 circles. Firmly press edges together to seal.
- Boil the lightly salted water in a large pot. Drop pierogi in a few at a time. Boil for about 2 mins until it floats on the surface. Remove using a slotted spoon when pierogi is cooked. Rinse until cold. Put aside.
- In a large skillet, melt remaining quarter cup of butter over medium-high heat. Put in boiled pierogi. Cook on both sides for about 5 mins until golden brown and hot. Enjoy immediately.

Nutrition Information

- Calories: 116 calories;
- Total Carbohydrate: 13.5 g
- Cholesterol: 26 mg
- Total Fat: 4.3 g
- Protein: 5.5 g
- Sodium: 72 mg

---

138. Pierogi II

"Vereneke (dough pockets) with cottage cheese filling and served with creamy gravy."
Serving: 12 | Prep: 20m | Ready in: 30m

Ingredients

- 2 eggs
- 1 cup milk
- 3 cups all-purpose flour
- 1 tsp. salt
- 2 cups drained cottage cheese
- 2 eggs
- 1 pinch salt

Direction

- Mix together the salt, flour, milk, and 2 eggs in a medium bowl to form a soft dough. Roll the dough thinly enough to have about twelve 4-inch squares. In the meantime, boil a big pot of lightly salted water.
- Mix together the salt, 2 eggs and cheese in a medium bowl. Fill each dough squares with the cottage cheese mixture. To seal, pinch the sides together then put it in the boiling water. Cook until the squares float on top of the water, or for about 8-10 minutes.

Nutrition Information

- Calories: 186 calories;
- Total Carbohydrate: 25.9 g
- Cholesterol: 69 mg
- Total Fat: 4.1 g
- Protein: 10.7 g
- Sodium: 378 mg

139. Pierogi III

"A classic Czechoslovakian recipe, cooked pierogi with melted butter and sautéed onions."
Serving: 30 | Prep: 1h | Ready in: 1h5m

Ingredients

- 2 slices bacon
- 1 (20 oz.) can sauerkraut, drained and rinsed
- 1 tsp. onion powder
- 3 tbsps. bacon grease
- 3 eggs
- 1/4 cup half-and-half cream
- 1/2 tsp. salt
- 3/4 cup milk
- 1/4 cup butter, softened
- 5 1/2 cups all-purpose flour
- 1/4 cup butter, melted
- 1 egg, beaten

Direction

- In a big, deep skillet, put the bacon. Over medium high heat, let cook till equally brown. Drain, keeping bacon grease, crumble and put aside.
- Mix bacon grease, crumbled bacon, onion powder and sauerkraut in medium bowl. Mix thoroughly; put aside.
- Using electric mixer, whisk together a quarter cup of butter, milk, salt, half-and-half and 3 eggs in big bowl. To create a soft dough, mix in the flour. Put cover; in a warm place, allow to rest for 5 minutes. Oil dough and hands with butter; on a floured surface, knead for 10 minutes. Split dough into 4 portions, and oil each using butter to avoid drying out.
- Melt leftover a quarter cup of butter; whisk leftover egg, then put together butter and egg; put aside. Unroll a portion of dough to a thickness of 1/8 inch. Cut out 4-inch rounds using glass or round cutter. In the middle of every circle, put a tbsp. sauerkraut filling. With egg and butter mixture, brush edges of round, fold in 1/2 and pinch edges together to secure. Repeat with the rest of the portions of dough.
- Boil a big pot of water. Let the pierogi cook for 5 minutes, or till they rise to the surface.

Nutrition Information

- Calories: 145 calories;
- Total Carbohydrate: 18.8 g
- Cholesterol: 36 mg
- Total Fat: 6 g
- Protein: 3.9 g
- Sodium: 220 mg

140. Pierogies

"Try this and you won't regret!"
Serving: 16 | Prep: 1h | Ready in: 2h

Ingredients

- 1 (16 oz.) container sour cream
- 3 cups all-purpose flour
- 2 cups cold mashed potatoes
- 1/2 cup butter
- 2 large onions, chopped

Direction

- In large bowl, put sour cream. Create a dough by mixing in the flour. On floured surface, roll dough out about 1/16-inch thickness. Using a glass or cookie cutter, cut rounds about 3 1/2-inch across. Create more rounds by rerolling unused dough up to four times. After that, the dough will be hard to work with.

- In middle of each dough round, put about one tsp. mashed potatoes. Fold over into the half-moon shape, use a fork to press and seal edges. Put filled pierogies aside under the towel to avoid drying.
- In a large skillet, melt butter over medium-low heat. Cook while stirring onions for 4-5 mins until translucent. Discard cooked onions. Put aside, retaining the butter in skillet.
- Boil water in a large saucepan. Drop a few filled pierogies carefully at a time into boiling water. After floating on surface, let pierogies gently boil for about 4 mins.
- In the skillet, reheat the butter over medium heat. Scoop pierogies gently out of water (they are easily broken). Put them into skillet for about 3 mins to brown on the bottom. On the buttered baking sheet, place fried pierogies. Sprinkle cooked onions over. Keep them warm on low setting in oven till served.

Nutrition Information

- Calories: 226 calories;
- Total Carbohydrate: 25.5 g
- Cholesterol: 28 mg
- Total Fat: 12.1 g
- Protein: 4.1 g
- Sodium: 136 mg

141. Pork Stroganoff

""Beef stroganoff is the norm. Why not try pork stroganoff? It's equally great, if not better. This delicious recipe entails onions, mushrooms and pork in a rich sour cream sauce!""
Serving: 4

Ingredients

- 4 (1 1/4 inch) thick pork chops
- 2 tbsps. vegetable oil
- 1 onion, thinly sliced
- 1/4 lb. fresh mushrooms, sliced
- 1/4 cup water
- 2 tsps. prepared mustard

- 1/2 tsp. salt
- 1/2 cup sour cream
- 2 tbsps. chopped fresh parsley, for garnish

Direction

- In a big skillet over medium-high heat, heat oil and cook chops on both sides until well browned. Move the chops away from the pan and set aside.
- Insert mushrooms and onion into the skillet and cook until tender, stirring from time to time. Move the chops back into the skillet then stir salt, mustard and water in. Increase the heat to high and bring it to a boil. Adjust the heat to low and cover it up. Let it simmer for 1 hour. Transfer chops to a warm platter.
- Add sour cream into the skillet and heat thoroughly, being careful not to boil. Empty the sauce over pork chops and garnish with parsley. Serve.

Nutrition Information

- Calories: 299 calories;
- Total Carbohydrate: 4.8 g
- Cholesterol: 82 mg
- Total Fat: 19 g
- Protein: 26.9 g
- Sodium: 384 mg

142. Potato And Cheese Pierogi

"The best treat for your family!"
Serving: 60 | Prep: 2h | Ready in: 2h10m

Ingredients

- 6 cups all-purpose flour
- 3 eggs
- 1 pinch salt
- water as needed
- 5 lbs. potatoes, peeled
- 1 lb. processed cheese, cubed
- salt and pepper to taste
- onion salt to taste

Direction

- Bring a large pot of salted water to a boil. Put in potatoes. Cook for about 15 mins until tender yet still firm, then drain.
- Combine salt, eggs and flour. Mix in little water at a time until the dough has become somewhat stiff. Roll the dough in small sections, about 1/4-inch in thickness. Create circle cuts with a drinking glass or large biscuit cutter.
- For the filling: Mix onion salt, pepper, salt, cheese and potatoes together. Fill 1-2 tbsps. potato mixture onto each, fold over then seal the edges. To cook, boil water in a large pot, dropping in 1 at a time carefully, stir once. Once they float to top, they are done.

Nutrition Information

- Calories: 97 calories;
- Total Carbohydrate: 15.4 g
- Cholesterol: 15 mg
- Total Fat: 2.3 g
- Protein: 3.5 g
- Sodium: 101 mg

143. Pumpkin Pasta

"Tasty!"
Serving: 3 | Prep: 5m | Ready in: 20m

Ingredients

- 6 oz. whole wheat penne pasta
- 3/4 cup pumpkin puree
- 3/4 cup low sodium chicken broth
- 1/4 cup nonfat milk
- 1 tsp. margarine
- 1/4 tsp. onion powder
- 1/4 tsp. ground black pepper
- 1/4 tsp. salt
- 1 pinch ground cloves
- 1 pinch ground nutmeg
- 1 pinch ground cinnamon
- 1 pinch ground ginger

- 1/4 cup grated Parmesan cheese, plus more for serving

Direction

- Bring a large pot of lightly salted water to a rolling boil over high heat. Stir in penne when water is boiling. Bring back to a boil. Cook pasta, uncovered, for about 11 mins until pasta has cooked through yet still firm to bite, stirring occasionally. Drain well in a colander placed in sink.
- In a large skillet, heat ginger, cinnamon, nutmeg, cloves, salt, black pepper, onion powder, margarine, milk, chicken broth and pumpkin puree over low heat for about 5 mins until heated through. Stir in drained pasta. Toss with Parmesan cheese.

Nutrition Information

- Calories: 255 calories;
- Total Carbohydrate: 45.3 g
- Cholesterol: 7 mg
- Total Fat: 4.4 g
- Protein: 12.4 g
- Sodium: 500 mg

144. Pumpkin Pasta With Cheddar

""The vegetables are heavy on this uncommon dish, and not so much on pasta.""
Serving: 8 | Prep: 15m | Ready in: 55m

Ingredients

- 6 oz. macaroni
- 1 tsp. olive oil
- 1/2 onion, chopped
- 1 tbsp. minced garlic
- 1 small zucchini, peeled and thinly sliced
- 1 tsp. dried sage
- 1/2 tsp. dried thyme
- 1 (15 oz.) can pumpkin puree
- 1 cup ricotta cheese
- 1/4 cup white wine
- 1/2 cup shredded Cheddar cheese

Direction

- Set the oven to 325°F or 165°C for preheating.
- Boil the lightly salted water in a large pot. Add the elbow macaroni into the boiling water and cook for 8 minutes, stirring occasionally until tender but firm to the bite; drain. Transfer the macaroni into the 2-qt casserole dish.
- Put oil in a large skillet and heat it. Stir in onion and garlic and cook for 5-6 minutes until softened. Add the sage, thyme, and zucchini. Cook for 3-4 minutes, stirring well until the zucchini is slightly tender. Mix in ricotta cheese, white wine, and pumpkin into the zucchini mixture.
- Working in batches, pour the pumpkin mixture into the blender, not more than half full. Cover the blender, holding the lid down, and pulse it a few times before blending it until smooth.
- Sprinkle pasta with the Cheddar cheese. Mix in pumpkin sauce. Use an aluminum foil to cover the dish.
- Let it bake inside the preheated oven for about 25 minutes until bubbling.

Nutrition Information

- Calories: 146 calories;
- Total Carbohydrate: 22.5 g
- Cholesterol: 7 mg
- Total Fat: 3.5 g
- Protein: 5.5 g
- Sodium: 176 mg

145. Purple Cauliflower Pasta

"The flavor of this dish is so amazing!"
Serving: 4 | Prep: 20m | Ready in: 40m

Ingredients

- 2 cups uncooked rotini pasta
- 1/4 cup walnuts
- 2 tbsps. olive oil
- 1 clove garlic, sliced
- 1/2 head purple cauliflower, cut into small florets
- 1/2 tsp. kosher salt
- 1 tbsp. balsamic vinegar
- 1 pinch red pepper flakes
- 2 tsps. chopped fresh rosemary
- 1/2 tsp. kosher salt
- 2 pinches grated Parmesan cheese, or to taste

Direction

- Boil the lightly salted water in a large pot. Cook rotini at a boil for about 8 mins until tender but firm to bite, then drain, saving half cup of the cooking water.
- Over medium-low heat, heat a small skillet. In the hot pan, place walnuts; continually cook while stirring for 3-5 mins until fragrant and toasted. Take away from the heat, then chop the walnuts.
- In a pan, heat olive oil over medium heat. Cook while stirring garlic for 2-3 mins in the hot oil, until golden. Take off garlic from the pan. Put aside.
- In the same pan, cook while stirring half tsp. of kosher salt and cauliflower over medium-high heat for 8 to 10 mins until the cauliflower is tender, stirring occasionally.
- Add the balsamic vinegar over the cauliflower. Cook while stirring the cauliflower for about one minute until the balsamic vinegar is reduced.
- Stir rosemary, red pepper flakes, cooked garlic and walnuts into the cauliflower mixture until combined well.
- Stir reserved half cup of cooking water and cooked rotini into the cauliflower mixture until blended well. Sprinkle cauliflower and rotini mixture with Parmesan cheese and half tsp. of kosher salt.

Nutrition Information

- Calories: 289 calories;
- Total Carbohydrate: 37.2 g
- Cholesterol: < 1 mg
- Total Fat: 12.6 g
- Protein: 8.3 g

- Sodium: 513 mg

146. Purple Pasta

"Budget-friendly, easy, and still tasty when reheated. Prepare this fast and simple dish for you to enjoy on your lazy days."
Serving: 6 | Prep: 10m | Ready in: 25m

Ingredients

- 1 (8 oz.) package rigatoni pasta
- 1 (12 oz.) can sliced beets, drained and diced
- 1 (10 oz.) can artichoke hearts, drained
- 2 tbsps. olive oil
- 1/4 tsp. dried basil, or to taste
- 1/4 tsp. dried oregano, or to taste

Direction

- Fill a large pot with lightly salted water and boil. Add the rigatoni in and cook for about 13 minutes, until al dente. Stir occasionally. Drain.
- Transfer the pasta into a bowl. Mix in oregano, basil, olive oil, artichoke hearts and beets thoroughly. Serve.

Nutrition Information

- Calories: 217 calories;
- Total Carbohydrate: 36.4 g
- Cholesterol: 0 mg
- Total Fat: 5.5 g
- Protein: 7.2 g
- Sodium: 399 mg

147. Quick Creamy Spinach And Tomato Pasta

"This dish makes a good dish even if it only has a few ingredients."
Serving: 4 | Prep: 5m | Ready in: 20m

Ingredients

- 8 oz. angel hair pasta
- 1 (14.5 oz.) can diced tomatoes
- 2 cups baby spinach leaves
- 1/2 cup sour cream
- 1 tbsp. prepared basil pesto (optional)

Direction

- In a big pot, let lightly salted water boil. Put pasta and cook until tender for 3 to 4 minutes. Drain it.
- Over medium heat, combine spinach and tomatoes in a saucepan. Stir in the pesto and sour cream when the spinach is starting to wilt. Toss drained pasta with sauce. Immediately serve.

Nutrition Information

- Calories: 263 calories;
- Total Carbohydrate: 36 g
- Cholesterol: 14 mg
- Total Fat: 9.3 g
- Protein: 8.8 g
- Sodium: 330 mg

148. Quick Pasta Primavera

"Try this and you won't regret!"
Serving: 5

Ingredients

- 5 oz. dry fettuccine pasta
- 1/4 cup water
- 2 cups fresh sliced mushrooms
- 9 oz. frozen French-style green beans
- 1/2 cup chopped red bell pepper

- 1 clove garlic, minced
- 1/4 tsp. ground black pepper
- 1 (12 fluid oz.) can evaporated milk
- 4 tsps. cornstarch
- 1/2 cup shredded mozzarella cheese
- 1 large tomato, cut into wedges

Direction

- Boil the lightly salted water in a large pot. Put in pasta. Cook until al dente or 8-10 mins. Drain, then reserve.
- In the meantime, combine ground black pepper, garlic, green or red bell pepper, beans, mushrooms and water in a medium saucepan. Boil. Lower the heat, simmer, covered, until the vegetables become tender, for 4 mins; do not drain.
- Combine cornstarch and milk in a small bowl. Stir into the vegetable mixture. Cook while stirring over medium heat until bubbly and thickened. Cook while stirring for one more minute. Put in cheese, then stir until cheese is melted. Pour the sauce over the pasta. Decorate with the tomato wedges. Enjoy.

Nutrition Information

- Calories: 278 calories;
- Total Carbohydrate: 36.9 g
- Cholesterol: 31 mg
- Total Fat: 9.1 g
- Protein: 13.4 g
- Sodium: 156 mg

149. Quick Stuffed Tomatoes

""This recipe for stuffed tomatoes is very delicious.""
Serving: 4 | Prep: 25m | Ready in: 55m

Ingredients

- 4 large tomatoes
- 1 1/2 cups vegetable broth
- 1/2 cup sun-dried tomatoes, chopped
- 1 cup couscous

- 1/4 cup shredded nonfat mozzarella cheese
- 1/4 cup chopped fresh basil
- 2 tbsps. minced fresh mint leaves
- 1/4 tsp. ground black pepper

Direction

- Set the oven to 375°F (190°C) for preheating.
- Cut the fresh tomatoes in half crosswise. Scoop out their pulp and put aside. Place the tomato shells onto the paper towels, inverted, to allow them to drain.
- Boil the sun-dried tomatoes and broth in a small saucepan. Remove the pan from the heat and mix in couscous. Cover the pan and allow it to stand for 5 minutes.
- Mix in pepper, cheese, mint, and basil. Stir in tomato pulp gently.
- Arrange the tomato shells into the 11x7-inches baking pan. Spoon the couscous mixture into the shells. Make sure to press the mixture firmly into the shells. Let them bake at 190 degrees C (375 degrees F) inside the preheated oven for 25-30 minutes until heated through.

Nutrition Information

- Calories: 245 calories;
- Total Carbohydrate: 47.7 g
- Cholesterol: 1 mg
- Total Fat: 1.1 g
- Protein: 11.4 g
- Sodium: 284 mg

150. Restaurant Style Lasagna

""Simple but yummy recipe. An all-time favorite! Good in manicotti as well.""
Serving: 8 | Prep: 20m | Ready in: 1h10m

Ingredients

- 9 lasagna noodles
- 2 1/2 cups ricotta cheese
- 1 1/2 cups mozzarella cheese, shredded
- 1/4 cup grated Parmesan cheese
- 2 eggs, beaten

- 1/2 lb. lean ground beef
- 2 1/2 tsps. dried oregano
- 1 1/2 tsps. dried basil
- 1/2 tsp. garlic powder
- 2 tsps. white sugar
- salt and pepper to taste
- 3 (6.5 oz.) cans tomato sauce

Direction

- Let a big pot of water with a little bit of salt boil. Put the lasagna noodles in the boiling water and cook 8-10 minutes until al dente then drain the noodles.
- Preheat the oven at 350°F (175°C).
- For the filling: Mix eggs, parmesan cheese, mozzarella cheese and ricotta cheese together in a bowl.
- For the sauce: Cook the ground beef in a frying pan until brown and fully cooked then drain excess oil. Mix the cooked ground beef, salt, pepper, sugar, oregano, basil, garlic powder and tomato sauce together in the frying pan. Cook and give it a stir.
- In a 13x9-inch pan, make 3 layers of cooked lasagna noodles, filling and sauce. Put mozzarella cheese on top but this is optional. Put in the preheated oven and bake for 40 minutes. Allow it to cool down for 10 minutes before slicing.

Nutrition Information

- Calories: 259 calories;
- Total Carbohydrate: 25.7 g
- Cholesterol: 79 mg
- Total Fat: 10 g
- Protein: 17.3 g
- Sodium: 567 mg

151.Ricotta Spaghetti

"This recipe is sure to become your favorite!"
Serving: 6 | Prep: 10m | Ready in: 25m

Ingredients

- 3/4 lb. spaghetti
- 1 clove garlic, minced
- 1 cup part-skim ricotta cheese
- 2 tsps. chopped fresh basil
- salt and ground black pepper to taste
- 2 tbsps. grated Parmesan cheese

Direction

- Fill lightly salted water in a large pot and bring to a rolling boil over high heat. Stir in the spaghetti when water is boiling, then bring back to a boil. Cook pasta, uncovered, for about 12 mins, stirring occasionally, until pasta has cooked through yet still firm to bite. Let it drain well in a colander placed in the sink, saving two tbsps. cooking water.
- In a saucepan, stir basil, ricotta, and garlic over medium-low for about 4 mins until hot. Season with pepper and salt to taste; stir in reserved water from cooking the pasta and spaghetti. Sprinkle with the Parmesan cheese. Enjoy.

Nutrition Information

- Calories: 275 calories;
- Total Carbohydrate: 44.7 g
- Cholesterol: 14 mg
- Total Fat: 4.6 g
- Protein: 12.8 g
- Sodium: 80 mg

152. Roasted Cherry Tomatoes With Angel Hair

"This delish is made out of fresh cherry tomatoes and basil."
Serving: 2 | Prep: 20m | Ready in: 59m

Ingredients

- 1 (10 oz.) basket cherry tomatoes, halved
- 1 tbsp. olive oil
- 1 tsp. minced garlic
- salt and ground black pepper to taste
- 4 oz. angel hair pasta
- 3 basil leaves, cut into thin strips, or more to taste
- 1 dash red pepper flakes
- 2 tbsps. fresh grated Parmesan cheese, or to taste (optional)

Direction

- Preheat oven to 190 °C or 375 °F.
- In a bowl, combine pepper, salt, garlic, olive oil and tomatoes until mixed well, then, spread mixture on a shallow-sided baking sheet.
- In the preheated oven, bake for 25 to 30 minutes until tomatoes are wrinkled and soft.
- In a big pot, let lightly salted water boil. In the boiling water, cook angel hair pasta 4 to 5 minutes until cooked through but firm to the bite, stirring occasionally. Drain but reserve a small amount of cooking water.
- In a small saucepan, spoon tomatoes with their juices over. Put red pepper flakes and basil. Over thin tomato mixture, mix in reserved cooking water to desired consistency. Over low heat, cook and stir for about 5 minutes until warmed. Stir pasta in. Put parmesan cheese on top. Serve.

Nutrition Information

- Calories: 287 calories;
- Total Carbohydrate: 39.8 g
- Cholesterol: 4 mg
- Total Fat: 10.6 g
- Protein: 11.2 g
- Sodium: 283 mg

153. Roasted Veggies With Couscous

""This light couscous is dressed with balsamic vinegar and olive oil. It's a perfect vegetarian dish for summer or winter.""
Serving: 8 | Prep: 10m | Ready in: 40m

Ingredients

- 1 large zucchini, thickly sliced
- 4 oz. button mushrooms, quartered
- 1 red bell pepper, chopped
- 1 tbsp. olive oil
- 3 cups water
- 1 tsp. salt
- 2 tbsps. olive oil
- 2 cups couscous
- 2 tbsps. balsamic vinegar

Direction

- Set the grill to high heat for preheating, either indoor or outdoor.
- Coat the vegetables lightly with olive oil. Arrange the vegetables on the grill. Let them cook, turning over occasionally until the vegetables are just tender.
- Meanwhile, boil couscous, 1 tbsp. of olive oil, water, and salt in a large pot. Remove the pot from the heat after boiling. Allow it to stand for 5 minutes. Use a fork to fluff it once done. Allow the couscous to cool to room temperature.
- Spoon the couscous on a plate. Place the veggies on its top. Drizzle over the balsamic vinegar and a small amount of olive oil.

Nutrition Information

- Calories: 224 calories;
- Total Carbohydrate: 36.8 g
- Cholesterol: 0 mg

- Total Fat: 5.5 g
- Protein: 6.6 g
- Sodium: 301 mg

154. S.o.b. (south Of The Border) Casserole

"This dish will satisfy anyone."
Serving: 4 | Prep: 15m | Ready in: 35m

Ingredients

- 1/2 lb. ground turkey
- 1/4 cup chopped onion
- 1 (16 oz.) can stewed tomatoes, undrained
- 1 (.75 oz.) packet brown gravy mix
- 1 tsp. chili powder, or to taste
- 1/2 cup frozen corn kernels
- 1/2 cup uncooked elbow macaroni
- 1 cup shredded lettuce
- 3 tbsps. sour cream
- 2 cups corn tortilla chips

Direction

- Boil the lightly salted water in small saucepan. Put in macaroni. Cook for about 6 mins until it is almost tender. Drain. Put aside.
- In a large pan, crumble the turkey set over medium heat. Cook while stirring until it is brown evenly, then drain. Put onion into the browned turkey meat. Cook for about 5 mins until the onion is tender. Stir in chili powder, gravy mix and tomatoes until they are combined. Mix in macaroni and corn. Cover and lower the heat to low. Simmer, stirring occasionally, for 10 mins.
- Arrange on a bed of tortilla chips to serve. Top with sour cream and shredded lettuce.

Nutrition Information

- Calories: 297 calories;
- Total Carbohydrate: 34.4 g
- Cholesterol: 47 mg
- Total Fat: 10.6 g

- Protein: 16.7 g
- Sodium: 606 mg

155. Sassy Spaghetti

"Your husband will love this recipe."
Serving: 8 | Prep: 15m | Ready in: 30m

Ingredients

- 1 (16 oz.) package spaghetti
- 1 tbsp. olive oil
- 1/2 onion, chopped
- 1 (15 oz.) can black beans, drained
- 1 (11 oz.) can sweet corn, drained
- 1 tbsp. ground cumin
- salt and pepper to taste
- 2 dashes hot sauce
- 3 tbsps. grated Parmesan cheese

Direction

- Boil the lightly salted water in a large pot. Put in pasta, cook until al dente for 8-10 mins, then drain.
- In a skillet, heat oil over medium heat. Stir in corn, beans, and onion. Season with pepper, salt, and cumin. Add a sprinkle of hot sauce over. Cook while stirring until the onion becomes tender. Toss with the cooked spaghetti. Add a sprinkle of the Parmesan cheese over. Enjoy.

Nutrition Information

- Calories: 251 calories;
- Total Carbohydrate: 46.4 g
- Cholesterol: 2 mg
- Total Fat: 3.5 g
- Protein: 8.2 g
- Sodium: 151 mg

156. Scallops And Spinach Over Pasta

""A recipe loved by many. This flavorful recipe is well balanced, low in fat, and yummy.""
Serving: 12 | Prep: 30m | Ready in: 1h

Ingredients

- 12 oz. spaghetti
- 3 lbs. bay scallops, raw
- 1 (10 oz.) package frozen chopped spinach, thawed
- 1 tbsp. fresh lemon juice
- 1 tbsp. olive oil
- 1/4 cup water
- garlic powder to taste
- salt and pepper to taste
- 1/4 cup grated Parmesan cheese

Direction

- Place lightly salted water in a big pot and make it boil. Cook in the pasta for 8-10 minutes or until it is al dente; strain.
- Stir-fry the spinach in olive oil in a medium skillet until heated well. Add water, garlic powder, and lemon juice.
- Stir in scallops then cook for 3 minutes or until it is done. Be cautious to avoid overcooking. Add pepper and salt to season.
- Transfer drained spaghetti into a dish then pour the sauce and scallops on top. Place grated Parmesan cheese on top to serve.

Nutrition Information

- Calories: 228 calories;
- Total Carbohydrate: 24.8 g
- Cholesterol: 39 mg
- Total Fat: 3 g
- Protein: 24.2 g
- Sodium: 227 mg

157. Seasoned Orzo And Black Beans

"A simple, quick, and easy dish that can be enjoyed on its own."
Serving: 6 | Prep: 20m | Ready in: 25m

Ingredients

- 6 cups water
- 1 cup uncooked orzo pasta
- 1 (16 oz.) package frozen mixed vegetables
- 1 (15 oz.) can black beans, rinsed and drained
- 3 tbsps. butter
- 1/2 tsp. dried tarragon
- 1/2 tsp. dried thyme
- salt to taste
- ground black pepper to taste

Direction

- Mix water and pasta in a 4-qt. pot. On medium-high heat, cook pasta for 4-6mins, until the mixture fully boils. Keep on cooking for 8-10mins while mixing from time to time, until the pasta is tender.
- Mix in frozen vegetables, then cover; turn to medium-low heat. Cook for 2-4mins, until the veggies are crisp-tender; avoid overcooking. Drain the vegetables.
- Mix in thyme, tarragon, butter or margarine and beans. Keep on cooking until completely heated. Sprinkle pepper and salt to taste.

Nutrition Information

- Calories: 295 calories;
- Total Carbohydrate: 47.3 g
- Cholesterol: 15 mg
- Total Fat: 7.2 g
- Protein: 11.5 g
- Sodium: 294 mg

158. Sesame Pasta

"This side dish with Asian flair is so fast to make."
Serving: 4 | Prep: 10m | Ready in: 15m

Ingredients

- 1 tbsp. sesame oil
- 8 oz. dry fettuccine pasta
- 1/2 tsp. soy sauce
- 2 green onions, chopped
- 3/4 cup fresh bean sprouts
- 1 pinch cayenne pepper
- 1 pinch ground white pepper
- 1 pinch garlic powder
- 1 tbsp. toasted sesame seeds

Direction

- Break fettuccine noodles in half and add into a big pot of boiling salted water. Cook till al dente, drain off and wash.
- In a wok or a skillet on medium heat, heat the oil. Put in pasta, garlic powder, pepper, cayenne, bean sprouts, green onions and soy sauce. Mix and cook for 2 - 3 minutes. Move to the serving dishes and use toasted sesame seeds to decorate.

Nutrition Information

- Calories: 254 calories;
- Total Carbohydrate: 43.4 g
- Cholesterol: 0 mg
- Total Fat: 5.9 g
- Protein: 8.7 g
- Sodium: 43 mg

159. Sharktooth Pasta

"Bowtie pasta in a creamy, kid-friendly sauce."
Serving: 4 | Prep: 12m | Ready in: 24m

Ingredients

- 8 oz. dry farfalle (bow tie) pasta

- 1 (10.75 oz.) can condensed cream of chicken soup
- 1/4 cup milk
- 2 tbsps. shredded Cheddar cheese

Direction

- Boil a big pot of lightly salted water. Put pasta and cook till al dente or for 8 to 10 minutes; let drain.
- Put pasta back to pot; mix in milk and soup. Cook and mix over medium heat till heated through. Put in cheese; let cook and mix just till cheese is melted. Serve while hot.

Nutrition Information

- Calories: 294 calories;
- Total Carbohydrate: 47 g
- Cholesterol: 12 mg
- Total Fat: 7.4 g
- Protein: 10.8 g
- Sodium: 534 mg

160. Shrimp Florentine With Zoodles

"This shrimp dinner uses zoodles in place of pasta."
Serving: 4 | Prep: 10m | Ready in: 25m

Ingredients

- 1 tbsp. butter
- 1 tbsp. extra-virgin olive oil
- 2 zucchini, cut into noodle-shape strands
- 1/2 large yellow onion, minced
- 1 tbsp. chopped garlic
- 1/2 tsp. kosher salt
- 2 tbsps. butter
- 1 lb. large shrimp, peeled and deveined
- 1 tsp. minced garlic
- 1 (6 oz.) bag baby spinach
- 1 tbsp. fresh lemon juice
- 1 tsp. red pepper flakes
- 1/2 tsp. kosher salt
- 1/2 tsp. freshly ground black pepper

Direction

- In a big frying pan, heat olive oil and 1 tbsp. butter on medium; stir and cook onion, 1/2 tsp. salt, zoodles (zucchini noodles), and chopped garlic until onion is translucent and zoodles are tender, 5 minutes. Put the zoodle mixture in a bowl.
- In the same pan, heat 2 tbsps. butter; add minced garlic and shrimp, cook, and stir until shrimp turns pink, 3-4 minutes. Add pepper, red pepper flakes, spinach, 1/2 tsp. salt, and lemon juice; stir and cook for 3-4 minutes until spinach starts wilting. Add the zoodle mixture; stir and cook for 2-3 minutes or until cooked through.

Nutrition Information

- Calories: 229 calories;
- Total Carbohydrate: 7.1 g
- Cholesterol: 195 mg
- Total Fat: 13.4 g
- Protein: 21 g
- Sodium: 781 mg

161. Simmering Marinara With Brie

"Yummy!"
Serving: 4 | Prep: 5m | Ready in: 55m

Ingredients

- 1 tbsp. olive oil
- 6 cloves garlic, minced
- 2 lbs. roma (plum) tomatoes, chopped
- 1/2 cup chopped fresh basil
- 8 oz. Brie cheese

Direction

- In a large skillet, heat olive oil over medium heat. Sauté the garlic but don't let brown. Stir in 1/2 basil and tomatoes. Lower the heat; simmer for 45 mins.
- Mix in the remaining basil. Discard rind from Brie. Put into pan. Let cheese melt without

stirring; combine by stirring. Take away from the heat. Enjoy sauce immediately.

Nutrition Information

- Calories: 268 calories;
- Total Carbohydrate: 10.8 g
- Cholesterol: 57 mg
- Total Fat: 19.6 g
- Protein: 14.2 g
- Sodium: 369 mg

162. Simple Smoky Penne And Meatballs

"This classic penne and meatballs recipe is twisted by BBQ sauce."
Serving: 6 | Prep: 5m | Ready in: 15m

Ingredients

- 1 box Barilla® Pronto™ Penne
- 3 cups water
- 10 frozen meatballs
- 1 cup Barilla® Marinara sauce
- 1/2 cup prepared BBQ sauce
- Salt and black pepper to taste
- 1/4 cup green onions, sliced
- 1/2 cup Cheddar cheese, grated
- 1/2 cup cilantro

Direction

- Add whole box of pasta to a big skillet (about 12-in. in diameter).
- Add 3 cups of cold water to the pan, making sure that the water covers the pasta.
- Switch the burner to high and set up your timer to 10 minutes (you can add a little salt to taste if desired).
- Put in meatballs after 5 minutes then mix to combine.
- When at the last minute of cooking, pour in both sauces and use pepper and salt to season; fold to combine.

- Take the skillet out of the heat and add cilantro, cheese and onions on top. Serve instantly.

Nutrition Information

- Calories: 171 calories;
- Total Carbohydrate: 11.1 g
- Cholesterol: 49 mg
- Total Fat: 9.2 g
- Protein: 10.3 g
- Sodium: 381 mg

163. Simply Lasagna

""For an everyday meal or special events, it's quick and easy!"
Serving: 12 | Prep: 20m | Ready in: 1h35m

Ingredients

- 1 lb. ground beef
- 2 1/2 cups KRAFT Shredded Low-Moisture Part-Skim Mozzarella Cheese, divided
- 1 (15 oz.) container POLLY-O Natural Part Skim Ricotta Cheese
- 1/2 cup KRAFT Grated Parmesan Cheese, divided
- 1/4 cup chopped fresh parsley
- 1 egg, beaten
- 1 (24 oz.) jar spaghetti sauce
- 1 cup water
- 12 lasagna noodles, uncooked

Direction

- Turn oven to 350° F.
- Cook meat in big skillet over medium-high heat until brown. Combine ricotta cheese, 1 1/4 cups mozzarella, 1/4 cup Parmesan, egg and parsley until blended thoroughly; reserve.
- Drain the meat; return to pan. Stir spaghetti sauce in. Pour 1 cup of water in the empty sauce bottle; seal with lid and shake well. Put in meat mixture; stir to mix properly. Place 1 cup meat sauce on the base of 13x9-in. baking pan; layer with 3 noodles, third of ricotta

cheese mixture and 1 cup of meat sauce. Repeat the layers 2x times more. Put remaining pasta, sauce and cheese on top. Wrap the top with greased foil.
- Bake until heated completely, 1 hour; after 45 min. remove the foil. Let it sit 15 min. before slicing. Serve.

Nutrition Information

- Calories: 293 calories;
- Total Carbohydrate: 26.1 g
- Cholesterol: 61 mg
- Total Fat: 12.5 g
- Protein: 17.8 g
- Sodium: 514 mg

164. Singapore Noodle Curry Shrimp

"You only need one skillet for this!"
Serving: 6 | Prep: 15m | Ready in: 25m

Ingredients

- 2/3 cup chicken broth
- 1 tbsp. oyster sauce
- 1 1/2 tbsps. soy sauce
- 1 1/2 tsps. white sugar
- 3 tbsps. peanut oil
- 1 1/2 tsps. curry powder
- 1 clove garlic, minced
- 1 tsp. minced fresh ginger root
- 1 small red bell pepper, diced
- 1 small red onion, chopped
- 4 green onions, chopped into 1 inch pieces
- 1 (12 oz.) package frozen cooked cocktail shrimp
- 1 1/2 cups frozen baby peas
- 1/2 (8 oz.) package rice noodles, broken into 3 inch pieces and soaked

Direction

- Mix sugar, soy sauce, oyster sauce, and chicken broth in a small bowl then put aside.

- Heat oil in a big skillet on medium-high heat. Add ginger, garlic, and curry powder. Stir-fry for around 10 seconds. Add scallions, onions, and peppers then stir-fry for 3-5 minutes. Mix chicken stock mixture in then boil on high heat. Add peas and shrimp then cook until it's hot. Add the noodles then cook until thoroughly heated. Immediately serve.

Nutrition Information

- Calories: 231 calories;
- Total Carbohydrate: 25 g
- Cholesterol: 110 mg
- Total Fat: 7.6 g
- Protein: 14.8 g
- Sodium: 491 mg

165. Skillet Gnocchi With Chard & White Beans

"A delicious one-pan dinner featuring gnocchi, dark leafy greens, white beans, and diced tomatoes then topped with mozzarella."
Serving: 6 | Ready in: 30m

Ingredients

- 1 tbsp. extra-virgin olive oil
- 1 (16 oz.) package shelf-stable gnocchi (see Tip)
- 1 tsp. extra-virgin olive oil
- 1 medium yellow onion, thinly sliced
- 4 cloves garlic, minced
- 1/2 cup water
- 6 cups chopped chard leaves or spinach
- 1 (15 oz.) can diced tomatoes with Italian seasonings
- 1 (15 oz.) can white beans, rinsed
- 1/4 tsp. freshly ground pepper
- 1/2 cup shredded part-skim mozzarella cheese
- 1/4 cup finely shredded Parmesan cheese

Direction

- On medium heat, heat a tbsp. of oil in a big non-stick pan. Add and cook gnocchi while stirring frequently for 5-7mins until it begins to brown and plump; move to a bowl.
- Add onion and the remaining tsp. of oil into the pan. On medium heat, cook and stir for 2mins. Mix in water and garlic; cover. Cook for 4-6mins until the onion is soft; put chard or spinach in. Cook and stir for 1-2mins until it begins to wilt. Mix in pepper, beans, and tomatoes; simmer. Mix in gnocchi then scatter Parmesan and mozzarella; cover. Cook for about 3mins until the sauce bubbles and the cheese melts.

Nutrition Information

- Calories: 259 calories;
- Total Carbohydrate: 29.5 g
- Cholesterol: 23 mg
- Total Fat: 11.1 g
- Protein: 9.7 g
- Sodium: 505 mg

166. Spaghetti Italian

"Your family will enjoy this delicious dish!"
Serving: 6 | Prep: 20m | Ready in: 1h20m

Ingredients

- 1/2 lb. Italian sausage
- 4 (6.5 oz.) cans tomato sauce
- 1 (14.5 oz.) can diced tomatoes
- 2 bay leaves
- 1 tsp. Italian seasoning
- 1/2 tsp. garlic powder
- 1 tsp. dried basil
- 1 tsp. dried oregano
- salt and pepper to taste
- 1 (8 oz.) package spaghetti

Direction

- Brown sausage in a large skillet over medium heat, then drain. Put aside.
- In large saucepan, combine Italian sausage, pepper, salt, oregano, basil, garlic powder, Italian seasoning, bay leaves, diced tomatoes and tomato sauce over medium heat; mix well.
- Over medium-low heat, simmer at least 60 mins; it would be best if simmered all day.
- Boil the lightly salted water in a large pot. Put in pasta. Cook until al dente or 8-10 mins. Drain.
- Mix hot pasta with sauce. Enjoy.

Nutrition Information

- Calories: 275 calories;
- Total Carbohydrate: 38.5 g
- Cholesterol: 15 mg
- Total Fat: 8 g
- Protein: 12.2 g
- Sodium: 1069 mg

167. Spaghetti Tacos

"A yummy angel hair pasta dish that is fast and simple to make."
Serving: 12 | Prep: 5m | Ready in: 20m

Ingredients

- 1 (16 oz.) package angel hair pasta
- 1 (28 oz.) jar spaghetti sauce
- 1 (5.8 oz.) package crisp taco shells
- 1/4 cup grated Parmesan cheese

Direction

- Let a large kettle with slightly salted water come to a rolling boil on high heat, and stir in the angel hair pasta, then bring back to boiling. Cook while uncovered, stirring every so often, for 4-5 minutes until completely cooked but still firm to the bite. Use a colander to drain properly, setting on a sink.

- Place the pasta back into the kettle, pouring the sauce over them, and stir it through until reheated. Place taco shells, stacked, in a microwave oven, fanning the stack out into a circular shape and the edges are overlapping slightly. Cook on a high setting for 30 to 45 seconds until crispy and warm. Fill the warm taco shells with pasta mixture and sprinkle pasta filling of each shell with 1 tsp. of Parmesan cheese, then serve.

Nutrition Information

- Calories: 236 calories;
- Total Carbohydrate: 38.5 g
- Cholesterol: 3 mg
- Total Fat: 6.2 g
- Protein: 6.8 g
- Sodium: 425 mg

168. Spaghetti With Marinara Sauce

"Easy and quick!"
Serving: 8

Ingredients

- 1 lb. spaghetti
- 1 (28 oz.) can crushed tomatoes
- 1 (14.5 oz.) can diced tomatoes
- 1 (15 oz.) can tomato sauce
- 1 tbsp. minced garlic
- 2 tsps. white sugar
- 2 tsps. dried parsley
- 1 tsp. garlic powder
- 1/2 tsp. salt
- 1/4 tsp. dried oregano
- 1/4 tsp. dried basil
- 1/4 tsp. ground black pepper
- 1 1/2 tbsps. capers
- 1 pinch crushed red pepper flakes (optional)

Direction

- Combine ground black pepper, basil, oregano, salt, garlic powder, parsley, sugar, minced garlic, tomato sauce, diced tomatoes and crushed tomatoes in a large saucepan. If desired, add crushed red pepper and capers. Cover and boil.
- Lower heat; cover and simmer for 45-60 mins.
- When simmering time nears, cook the spaghetti in large pot with boiling salted water until al dente.
- Toss the spaghetti with the cooked sauce. Enjoy warm.

Nutrition Information

- Calories: 273 calories;
- Total Carbohydrate: 55.9 g
- Cholesterol: 0 mg
- Total Fat: 1.3 g
- Protein: 10.3 g
- Sodium: 716 mg

169. Speedy Spaghetti

"This one is a must-try!"
Serving: 4 | Prep: 15m | Ready in: 40m

Ingredients

- 1/2 lb. ground beef
- 1 small onion, chopped
- 2 (8 oz.) cans tomato sauce
- 1 1/2 cups water
- 1 1/2 tsps. salt
- 1 tsp. dried parsley
- 1/2 pinch dried basil
- 1/2 tsp. black pepper
- 4 oz. uncooked spaghetti

Direction

- In large pan, brown ground beef with onion over medium heat until no longer pink; drain.
- Stir in pepper, basil, parsley, salt, water and tomato sauce; mix well, then heat until the

sauce is boiled. Break the spaghetti in 1/2. Drop a little at a time into sauce. Turn to low, covered.
- Cook for about 20-25 mins until the spaghetti becomes tender. Avoid the noodles from sticking together and sticking to the pan by stirring occasionally. If noodles start to dry out and they are not cooked, pour in water, 1/2-1 cup.

Nutrition Information

- Calories: 252 calories;
- Total Carbohydrate: 28.9 g
- Cholesterol: 34 mg
- Total Fat: 8.5 g
- Protein: 15.4 g
- Sodium: 1535 mg

170. Spicy Korean Chicken And Ramen Noodle Packets

"A delicious dish that's spicy!"
Serving: 4 | Prep: 20m | Ready in: 45m

Ingredients

- 3 tbsps. gochujang (Korean chile paste)
- 3 tbsps. soy sauce
- 1/3 cup water
- 2 tbsps. sesame oil
- 1 1/2 tsps. sugar
- 2 boneless, skinless chicken breasts, thinly sliced
- 1 cup (1-inch) slices green onions
- 1 cup thinly sliced red cabbage
- 2 cups thinly sliced button mushrooms
- 1 zucchini, thinly sliced
- 2 (3 oz.) packages ramen noodles, cooked al dente
- Reynolds Wrap® Aluminum Foil

Direction

- Preheat an oven to 425°F.

- In a big bowl, mix sugar, sesame oil, water, soy sauce and gochujang till combined.
- Add cooked ramen noodles, zucchini, mushrooms, cabbage, green onions and sliced chicken into big bowl with gochujang mixture; toss to coat.
- On a table, put 1 1/2-2 feet Reynolds wrap aluminum long sheet of foil. In middle of foil, put 1/4 ramen noodle mixture. Fold ends up then outside to make a foil packet.
- Repeat it thrice. On cookie sheet tray, put foil packets.
- Bake for 25 minutes in the oven till chicken is cooked through.

Nutrition Information

- Calories: 193 calories;
- Total Carbohydrate: 13.3 g
- Cholesterol: 29 mg
- Total Fat: 9.4 g
- Protein: 14.8 g
- Sodium: 1341 mg

171.Spicy Pasta

"It's easy and quick to make a pasta dish."
Serving: 6 | Prep: 10m | Ready in: 30m

Ingredients

- 1 (12 oz.) package rotini pasta
- 1 tbsp. vegetable oil
- 1 clove garlic, crushed
- 1 tsp. dried basil
- 1 tsp. Italian seasoning
- 1 onion, diced
- 2 red chile peppers, seeded and chopped
- 1 (14.5 oz.) can diced tomatoes
- 3 drops hot pepper sauce
- salt and ground black pepper to taste

Direction

- Boil the lightly salted water in a large pot. In the boiling water, cook pasta until al dente or for 8-10 mins, then drain.
- In the meantime, in a saucepan, heat oil over medium heat. Sauté basil with garlic and the Italian seasoning for 2-3 mins. Mix in chiles and onion, then cook until the onion becomes tender. Mix in the hot sauce and tomatoes, then simmer until heated through or for 5 mins. Toss with cooked pasta. Add pepper and salt to season.

Nutrition Information

- Calories: 134 calories;
- Total Carbohydrate: 22.5 g
- Cholesterol: 0 mg
- Total Fat: 2.8 g
- Protein: 4.4 g
- Sodium: 117 mg

172. Spicy Tuna Vegetable Bake

"A special tuna casserole."
Serving: 8 | Prep: 20m | Ready in: 1h18m

Ingredients

- 2 cups whole wheat rotini pasta
- 1 (10.75 oz.) can low-sodium cream of mushroom soup
- 1/2 (8 oz.) container sour cream
- 1 tbsp. red pepper flakes
- 1 tsp. garlic powder
- 1 tsp. ground black pepper
- 1/2 tsp. celery salt
- 2 (5 oz.) cans tuna, drained
- 1 cup sliced fresh mushrooms
- 1 cup thinly sliced carrots
- 1 cup 1-inch pieces fresh green beans
- 1/2 cup diced red onion
- 1 cup grated Colby-Monterey Jack cheese

Direction

- Preheat an oven to 200°C/400°F.
- Boil a big pot with lightly salted water. Cook rotini for 8 minutes till tender yet firm to chew; drain.
- In a bowl, mix celery salt, black pepper, garlic powder, red pepper flakes, sour cream and soup. Mix red onion, green beans, carrots, mushrooms, tuna and rotini in.
- Put in a casserole dish. Evenly sprinkle Colby-Monterey Jack cheese on top.
- In preheated oven, bake for 45 minutes till heated through.

Nutrition Information

- Calories: 268 calories;
- Total Carbohydrate: 28.9 g
- Cholesterol: 34 mg
- Total Fat: 10 g
- Protein: 17.9 g
- Sodium: 407 mg

173. Spinach And Black Bean Pasta

"A very easy and tasty vegetarian pasta dish."
Serving: 8 | Prep: 15m | Ready in: 45m

Ingredients

- 1 (16 oz.) package whole wheat rotini pasta
- 1 1/2 cups vegetable broth
- 2 1/2 cups chopped fresh spinach
- 1/2 cup chopped red onion
- 1 clove garlic, chopped
- 1/2 tsp. cayenne pepper
- salt and pepper to taste
- 1 (15 oz.) can black beans, drained and rinsed
- 1 cup frozen chopped broccoli
- 1 cup diced tomatoes
- 2 oz. freshly grated Parmesan cheese

Direction

- Boil the lightly salted water in a large pot. Put in rotini. Cook until al dente or 8-10 mins. Drain.
- In a large saucepan, boil vegetable broth over medium heat. Lower the heat, mix in pepper, salt, cayenne pepper, garlic, onion and spinach. Stir in broccoli and black beans. Continue to cook while stirring for 5-10 mins.
- Stir tomatoes into saucepan, keep on cooking until all the vegetables become tender or 10 mins. Serve over cooked pasta. Decorate with the Parmesan cheese.

Nutrition Information

- Calories: 279 calories;
- Total Carbohydrate: 51.1 g
- Cholesterol: 6 mg
- Total Fat: 3.2 g
- Protein: 14.9 g
- Sodium: 463 mg

174. Spinach And Pasta Shells

"An extremely easy pasta recipe."
Serving: 8

Ingredients

- 1 lb. seashell pasta
- 1 (10 oz.) package frozen chopped spinach
- 2 tbsps. olive oil
- 7 cloves garlic, minced
- 1 tsp. dried red pepper flakes (optional)
- salt to taste

Direction

- Boil a big pot of slightly salted water. Put in the spinach and pasta and cook till pasta is al dente, about 8 to 10 minutes; drain and set aside.
- In a big skillet, heat oil over moderate heat. Put in the red pepper flakes and garlic; sauté till garlic becomes pale gold, about 5 minutes.

In the skillet, put the spinach and cooked pasta and combine thoroughly. Add salt to season and toss; serve.

Nutrition Information

- Calories: 248 calories;
- Total Carbohydrate: 43.8 g
- Cholesterol: 0 mg
- Total Fat: 4.9 g
- Protein: 9 g
- Sodium: 30 mg

175. Spinach Garlic Pasta

"Skillet with pasta plus cooked chicken bits equals a heavenly quick and easy dish!"
Serving: 8

Ingredients

- 1 (16 oz.) package angel hair pasta
- 4 cloves garlic, minced
- 1 (10 oz.) package frozen chopped spinach, thawed
- 1 tbsp. olive oil

Direction

- In a large pot, boil water with salt and cook pasta until firm. Remove water.
- In a large skillet, heat oil. Toss in garlic and cook for 1 minute. Add in spinach and cooked pasta. Mix until well blended, then cook for about 2 minutes while stirring often. Ready to serve.

Nutrition Information

- Calories: 188 calories;
- Total Carbohydrate: 33 g
- Cholesterol: 0 mg
- Total Fat: 3.4 g
- Protein: 7.4 g
- Sodium: 142 mg

176. Spinach Kugel

"It's so easy to make."
Serving: 18 | Prep: 20m | Ready in: 1h30m

Ingredients

- 1 (16 oz.) package egg noodles
- 6 eggs, beaten
- 8 oz. butter, melted
- 1 (16 oz.) container sour cream
- 2 (1 oz.) envelopes dry onion soup mix
- 1 tsp. black pepper
- 4 (10 oz.) boxes frozen chopped spinach, thawed and drained

Direction

- Start preheating the oven to 350°F (175°C). Grease a 9x13 inches baking dish.
- Bring lightly salted water in a large pot to a rolling boil over high heat. Mix in egg noodles. Bring back to a boil. Cook pasta for about 5 mins until it has cooked through yet still firm to the bite. Drain well in a colander placed in the sink.
- In a large bowl, combine pepper, soup mix, sour cream, melted butter and eggs. Stir in drained spinach and cooked noodles. Spoon into the prepared baking dish.
- Bake in the preheated oven for about 1 hour until golden brown and hot. If kugel stars to brown too quickly, cover the dish with aluminum foil.

Nutrition Information

- Calories: 287 calories;
- Total Carbohydrate: 23.6 g
- Cholesterol: 113 mg
- Total Fat: 18.4 g
- Protein: 8.8 g
- Sodium: 432 mg

177. Spinach Noodle Casserole

"It's quick, easy but tasty!"
Serving: 8 | Prep: 45m | Ready in: 3h20m

Ingredients

- 8 oz. dry spinach noodles
- 2 tbsps. vegetable oil
- 1 1/2 cups sour cream
- 1/3 cup all-purpose flour
- 1 1/2 cups cottage cheese
- 4 green onions, minced
- 2 tsps. Worcestershire sauce
- 1 dash hot pepper sauce
- 2 tsps. garlic salt

Direction

- In a large pot, cook noodles in the salted boiling water until they are barely tender. Drain, then rinse under the cold water. Toss with the vegetable oil.
- In large bowl, combine flour and sour cream while the noodles are cooking. Mix well. Stir in garlic salt, hot pepper sauce, Worcestershire sauce, green onions and cottage cheese. Stir the noodles into the mixture. Grease inside of the slow cooker generously. Pour in the noodle mixture. Cook, covered, for 90-120 mins on high.

Nutrition Information

- Calories: 226 calories;
- Total Carbohydrate: 14.7 g
- Cholesterol: 35 mg
- Total Fat: 14.9 g
- Protein: 8.8 g
- Sodium: 669 mg

178. Spinach Ziti

"A colorful, simple pasta dish."
Serving: 6

Ingredients

- 8 oz. ziti pasta
- 1 (14.5 oz.) can Italian-style stewed tomatoes
- 1/8 tsp. crushed red pepper flakes
- 4 oz. fresh spinach, washed and chopped
- 2 oz. cream cheese
- 1/4 tsp. ground nutmeg

Direction

- Bring a large pot filled with salted water to a boil. Put in ziti and cook for about 12 minutes until tender yet still firm.
- In the meantime, combine hot pepper flakes and tomatoes in the medium sized non-reactive pan. Warm over medium-low heat; if necessary, break up the tomatoes.
- Drain the pasta, then put back to the hot pan. Put in nutmeg, cream cheese and spinach. Cook while stirring over low heat for 1-2 mins until the spinach is wilted. Pour tomato sauce over the spinach ziti. Stir and gently toss to mix.

Nutrition Information

- Calories: 196 calories;
- Total Carbohydrate: 32.7 g
- Cholesterol: 10 mg
- Total Fat: 4 g
- Protein: 6.7 g
- Sodium: 194 mg

179. Summer Penne Pasta

"This is a fantastic recipe on its own and you can easily customize it. Feel free to try different combinations of veggies or try out with different pasta shapes."
Serving: 8

Ingredients

- 1 (16 oz.) package penne pasta
- 1/3 lb. sliced green bell peppers
- 1/3 lb. sliced red bell peppers
- 1/3 lb. sliced yellow bell peppers
- 2 tbsps. olive oil
- 1 zucchini, sliced
- 1 yellow squash, sliced
- 6 oz. mushrooms, chopped
- 1 clove garlic, minced
- 2 medium tomato - peeled, seeded and chopped
- ground black pepper to taste
- salt to taste

Direction

- Cook the penne pasta in boiling salted water in a large pot until al dente. Then drain pasta and leave it slightly wet.
- As the pasta is cooking, rinse the bell peppers and slice them into 1/4-inch strips. Over medium heat, pour two tbsps. olive oil and sauté pepper in a large skillet until soft. Ensure the peppers are not browned.
- To the skillet, place in yellow squash and sliced zucchini and then sauté for two minutes. Add minced garlic and chopped mushrooms and then sauté for 2 more minutes while stirring often. Place in chopped tomatoes and take out from the heat source.
- Place pasta portions onto warmed plate. Top with sauce and sprinkle pepper and salt to taste.

Nutrition Information

- Calories: 264 calories;
- Total Carbohydrate: 47.6 g
- Cholesterol: 0 mg

- Total Fat: 5 g
- Protein: 9.5 g
- Sodium: 10 mg

180. Summer Tofu And Corn Pasta

"This simple pasta dish is just mouth-wateringly good."
Serving: 8 | Prep: 20m | Ready in: 45m

Ingredients

- 1 lb. spinach farfalle pasta
- 1 tbsp. canola oil
- 2 (8 oz.) packages firm silken tofu, drained and diced
- 3 tbsps. honey
- 1 tbsp. Dijon mustard
- 1 tsp. dry mustard
- 2 tsps. Old Bay® Seasoning
- 1 tsp. kosher salt
- freshly ground black pepper to taste
- 2 ears fresh sweet white corn, cut from the cob
- 1/3 cup nutritional yeast

Direction

- Allow a large pot filled with slightly salty water to boil, then add the pasta, cook for 13-15 minutes until the farfalle is al dente, then drain.
- In a wide saucepan, heat the oil over a medium heat, then stir in tofu. Mix in the Dijon mustard and honey, season with pepper, kosher salt, 1 tsp. of Old Bay® seasoning, and dry mustard. Cook while stirring until the tofu is fully coated.
- Mix the corn into the saucepan, then season with nutritional yeast and the leftover Old Bay seasoning, and cook until completely heated. Set aside to cool for 5 minutes before pouring over the cooked pasta to serve.

Nutrition Information

- Calories: 291 calories;
- Total Carbohydrate: 48.6 g

- Cholesterol: 41 mg
- Total Fat: 5.3 g
- Protein: 14.2 g
- Sodium: 466 mg

181.Sun-dried Tomato And Bow Tie Pasta

"You won't miss not having meat with this flavorful pasta dish that combines pesto sauce with red peppers, olive oil, and sun dried tomatoes. You can make this simple recipe even easier and faster with the use of 1/2 bottle of pre-made pesto instead of having to make your own. You can serve with a garnish of either Parmesan cheese or red pepper, depending on what you prefer."
Serving: 8

Ingredients

- 4 tbsps. dried basil
- 1 tbsp. minced pine nuts
- 1 tbsp. olive oil
- 3 oz. sun-dried tomatoes
- 1/8 cup olive oil
- 3 cloves garlic, minced
- 8 oz. fresh mushrooms, sliced
- 1/2 tsp. salt
- 1 tsp. cayenne pepper
- 1 (16 oz.) package bow tie pasta

Direction

- To make the pesto: Combine 1 tbsp. olive oil, pine nuts, and basil in a small mixing bowl.
- In another small bowl, blanch the sun dried tomatoes in boiling water for 30 seconds, then drain completely, and slice into small chunks.
- Sauté garlic with 1/8 cup olive oil in a large skillet over medium heat. Let simmer for 1 minute making sure that the garlic is not browned. Stir the mushrooms in and sauté until soft. Add the sun dried tomatoes, cayenne, salt, and pesto. Switch down the heat to low and let simmer.

- Let a big pot of salted water and pasta come to a boil. Cook until the pasta is al dente, and drain thoroughly.
- Toss pasta with the sauce in a big mixing bowl until the pasta is completely coated.

Nutrition Information

- Calories: 293 calories;
- Total Carbohydrate: 49.6 g
- Cholesterol: 0 mg
- Total Fat: 7.4 g
- Protein: 10.5 g
- Sodium: 371 mg

182. Super Mac

"It's so satisfying."
Serving: 8 | Prep: 15m | Ready in: 1h4m

Ingredients

- 1 tsp. coconut oil
- 1/2 cup panko bread crumbs
- 3 tbsps. grated pecorino Romano cheese
- 3 quarts water
- 1/2 tsp. salt
- 1 head cauliflower
- 4 carrots, sliced
- 1 cup vegetable broth
- 1/2 cup shredded Gruyere cheese
- 1/4 cup Neufchatel cheese
- 1 1/2 tsps. Dijon mustard
- 1/4 tsp. hot pepper sauce
- 8 oz. gluten-free penne pasta
- 1 cup shredded extra-sharp Cheddar cheese

Direction

- Start preheating the oven to 400°F (200°C). Grease a 2-qt baking dish.
- In small saucepan, melt the coconut oil. Put in panko. Toss for about 5 mins until toasted. Let cool to room temperature. Mix in the pecorino cheese.

- Boil the salted water in a large pot. Cut three cups of the small florets from the cauliflower head. Trim the remaining cauliflower into 2-inch pieces, including stem. Bring carrots and 2-inch cauliflower pieces to a boil for 10-12 mins until very tender. Strain, saving the water.
- In the bowl of a food processor, put hot pepper sauce, salt, Dijon mustard, Neufchatel cheese, Gruyere cheese and broth. Put in carrots and cooked cauliflower; puree until they become creamy and smooth.
- In a large pot, bring the water back to a boil. Put in pasta and boil for 3 mins. Put in the cauliflower florets and boil for one more minute. Strain the cauliflower and pasta, put back to the pot. Stir in cheese mixture and cauliflower. Spread prepared baking dish with pasta mixture. Add panko mixture and shredded Cheddar cheese over top.
- Bake in the preheated oven for 30-35 mins until bubbly and golden brown.

Nutrition Information

- Calories: 292 calories;
- Total Carbohydrate: 35.1 g
- Cholesterol: 36 mg
- Total Fat: 12.3 g
- Protein: 12.9 g
- Sodium: 514 mg

183. Syrian Spaghetti

"This dish will satisfy anyone."
Serving: 8 | Prep: 15m | Ready in: 1h15m

Ingredients

- 1 (16 oz.) package spaghetti
- 1 (8 oz.) can tomato sauce
- 1 (6 oz.) can tomato paste
- 1 tsp. ground cinnamon
- 1/4 cup vegetable oil
- salt and pepper to taste

Direction

- Start preheating the oven to 350°F (175°C). Grease 9x13 inches baking dish.
- Boil the lightly salted water in a large pot. Put in spaghetti. Cook until al dente or 8-10 mins. Drain, then stir in the pepper, salt, oil, cinnamon, tomato paste and tomato sauce. Place into the prepared dish.
- Bake for 60 mins in the preheated oven, or until the top becomes crunchy.

Nutrition Information

- Calories: 293 calories;
- Total Carbohydrate: 47.6 g
- Cholesterol: 0 mg
- Total Fat: 7.8 g
- Protein: 8.6 g
- Sodium: 318 mg

184. Tomato And Garlic Pasta

"This rich pasta dish is best done with fresh tomatoes. You can also use canned tomatoes, but either way, it would be well worth it. You can even make the sauce as fast as it will take to cook the pasta completely."
Serving: 4

Ingredients

- 1 (8 oz.) package angel hair pasta
- 2 lbs. tomatoes
- 4 cloves crushed garlic
- 1 tbsp. olive oil
- 1 tbsp. chopped fresh basil
- 1 tbsp. tomato paste
- salt to taste
- ground black pepper to taste
- 1/4 cup grated Parmesan cheese

Direction

- In a kettle, place the tomatoes in and cover with cold water, then boil. Drain and cover with more cold water. Peel and chop into small pieces.

- Cook pasta in a boiling large pot of salted water until al dente.
- Sauté the garlic in a large skillet with olive oil enough to cover the bottom of a pan. The garlic should not be browned but cooked until just opaque, then stir in tomato paste. Stir in tomatoes, pepper, and salt right after. Lower the heat, letting it simmer until pasta is ready, then add the basil.
- Drain pasta, and, without rinsing cold water, toss with a few tbsps. of olive oil before mixing in with the sauce. Decreasing the heat to the lowest setting, then keep warm without a lid on for 10 minutes or until ready to be served. Liberally garnish with freshly grated Parmesan cheese.
- If you want, you can also add in fresh mushrooms that have been quartered and sautéed with garlic, or you can add shoestring zucchini with the tomatoes.

Nutrition Information

- Calories: 260 calories;
- Total Carbohydrate: 41.9 g
- Cholesterol: 4 mg
- Total Fat: 6.8 g
- Protein: 10.3 g
- Sodium: 236 mg

185. Tomato Basil Spaghettini

"The strong taste of basil, garlic, and tomato combined with a fair amount of goat cheese will create an appetizing sauce to satisfy your senses."
Serving: 8 | Prep: 15m | Ready in: 25m

Ingredients

- 1 (16 oz.) package uncooked spaghettini
- 1 (14.5 oz.) can diced tomatoes with garlic
- 2 fresh tomatoes, chopped
- 1 cup fresh basil leaves
- 2 tbsps. minced garlic
- 2 tbsps. olive oil
- freshly ground black pepper to taste

- 1 lemon, juiced
- 4 oz. soft goat cheese

Direction

- Start boiling a large pot of lightly salted water. Add in pasta and cook until al dente, or for 8-10 minutes; then drain water.
- Mix pepper, olive oil, garlic, basil, fresh tomatoes, and the diced tomatoes in a food processor or a blender just until chunky.
- Carefully toss the mixture of tomato and cooked pasta in a bowl. Just before serving, dust the pasta with lemon juice and arrange goat cheese on top.

Nutrition Information

- Calories: 297 calories;
- Total Carbohydrate: 47.2 g
- Cholesterol: 7 mg
- Total Fat: 7.9 g
- Protein: 11 g
- Sodium: 306 mg

186. Tortellini Southwest

"A very tasty tortellini with your not so ordinary ingredients! Plus it's very easy to make!"
Serving: 4 | Prep: 5m | Ready in: 20m

Ingredients

- 9 oz. cheese-filled tortellini
- 1 1/2 cups spaghetti sauce
- 1 (4 oz.) can diced green chiles
- 1 tbsp. chopped fresh cilantro
- 1/8 tsp. ground cumin
- 1 cup shredded mozzarella cheese

Direction

- Boil salted water in a large pot and cook tortellini until al dente and drain thoroughly.
- Combine cumin, cilantro, green chilies and sauce in a 1-1/2 quart sized saucepan. Simmer for 5 minutes over medium-low heat.

- Transfer the tortellini to a chosen platter and evenly pour tomato sauce mixture over pasta. Sprinkle over sauce with cheese. Serve.

Nutrition Information

- Calories: 300 calories;
- Total Carbohydrate: 34.7 g
- Cholesterol: 34 mg
- Total Fat: 11.8 g
- Protein: 14.6 g
- Sodium: 1086 mg

187. Tuna And Red Pepper Sauce

"All you have to cook is the pasta!"
Serving: 8

Ingredients

- 8 oz. roasted red bell peppers, diced
- 1 (5 oz.) can tuna, drained
- 1/4 cup chopped parsley
- 1/4 cup olive oil
- 2 tsps. capers
- 2 tsps. minced garlic
- 1/2 tsp. salt
- 1/2 tsp. ground black pepper
- 1 lb. seashell pasta

Direction

- In a large pot of boiling salted water, add pasta and cook until al dente.
- Mix together pepper, salt, garlic, capers, olive oil, parsley, tuna and roasted red peppers in a large serving bowl.
- Drain the pasta and combine with tuna mixture right away.

Nutrition Information

- Calories: 293 calories;
- Total Carbohydrate: 43.3 g
- Cholesterol: 5 mg
- Total Fat: 8.4 g
- Protein: 12.1 g

- Sodium: 282 mg

188. Tuna Garden Casserole

"You can easily substitute veggies for what you have."
Serving: 8 | Prep: 30m | Ready in: 55m

Ingredients

- 8 oz. penne pasta
- 1 tbsp. olive oil
- 1 large onion, chopped
- 2 stalks celery, chopped
- 1 red bell pepper, chopped
- 2 cloves garlic, crushed
- salt, to taste
- ground black pepper, to taste
- 1/4 cup sherry
- 1/2 lb. kale, stems removed and leaves coarsely chopped
- 1 (14.1 oz.) can potato leek soup
- 1 cup vegetable broth
- 1 (5 oz.) can tuna packed in water, drained
- 1 cup shredded mozzarella cheese
- 1/3 cup herb seasoned bread crumbs

Direction

- Preheat an oven to 190°C/375°F. Grease a 2-qt. casserole dish lightly.
- Boil a big pot with salted water. Add penne pasta. Cook till al dente for 10 minutes; drain.
- Heat oil in big skillet/wok on medium high heat. Mix onion in; cook for 5 minutes. Mix bell pepper and celery in. Cook for 5 minutes more. Mix pepper, salt and garlic in; cook for 3 minutes. Put sherry in; mix kale in then cover. Lower heat to medium. Cook for 5 minutes, occasionally mixing, till kale wilts.
- Put wok mixture in big bowl. Mix tuna, vegetable broth, soup and cooked pasta in. Put mixture in prepped casserole dish. Put layer of mozzarella on top then a breadcrumbs layer. Bake in preheated oven, uncovered, for 25 minutes.

Nutrition Information

- Calories: 284 calories;
- Total Carbohydrate: 38.6 g
- Cholesterol: 21 mg
- Total Fat: 7.8 g
- Protein: 14.3 g
- Sodium: 472 mg

189. Tuna Lasagna Casserole

"A yummy recipe for classic tuna noodle casserole."
Serving: 12 | Prep: 35m | Ready in: 1h30m

Ingredients

- 12 lasagna noodles
- 1 tbsp. butter
- 3 tbsps. all-purpose flour
- 1/2 cup chicken broth
- 1 cup milk, divided
- 2 cloves garlic, minced
- 12 soda crackers
- 1 pinch Italian seasoning
- 3 (5 oz.) cans tuna, drained
- 1 1/2 cups frozen mixed vegetables
- 1 egg white
- 1/4 tsp. salt
- 1/2 cup grated Cheddar cheese
- 1/8 tsp. black pepper
- 1/2 cup grated Cheddar cheese

Direction

- Preheat oven to 175°C/350°F then grease a 9x13-in. baking dish.
- Fill big pot using lightly salted water; put on rolling boil on high heat. Mix lasagna in when water boils; boil again. Cook pasta, occasionally mixing, uncovered, for 8-9 minutes till pasta cooks through yet firm to chew. In a colander set in sink, drain well.
- Melt butter in a saucepan on medium low heat. Whisk flour in; mix for 5 minutes till mixture is light golden brown and paste-like. Whisk 1/2 milk and chicken broth slowly into flour mixture; simmer on medium heat. Mix and cook for 10-15 minutes till mixture is smooth and thick. Mix 1/2 minced garlic and leftover milk in.
- In resealable plastic bag, put soda crackers. Crush crackers finely; add Italian seasoning. Mix leftover minced garlic, 1/2 cup flour mixture, 1/4 cup cracker crumbs, 1/2 cup cheddar cheese, salt, egg white, mixed veggies and tuna in a big bowl.
- Spread thin white sauce layer on prepared baking sheet then a layer of lasagna noodles. Spread 1/3 tuna mixture on noodles. Repeat tuna and noodle layers 3 times more, topping with leftover flour mixture. Evenly sprinkle pepper on top of casserole. Use aluminum foil to cover.
- In preheated oven, bake for 35 minutes. Take out of oven. Use 1/2 cup cheddar cheese and leftover cracker crumbs on top. Put oven setting on broil; put casserole in oven. Broil for 2-3 minutes till lightly browned.

Nutrition Information

- Calories: 210 calories;
- Total Carbohydrate: 24 g
- Cholesterol: 24 mg
- Total Fat: 5.7 g
- Protein: 15.5 g
- Sodium: 222 mg

190. Tuna Mushroom Casserole

"This is a quick, and tasty dinner that is always a hit when served."
Serving: 6 | Prep: 10m | Ready in: 1h3m

Ingredients

- 2 cups bow tie pasta
- 2 (5 oz.) cans tuna, drained
- 1 (10 oz.) can mushrooms, drained
- 1 (10.5 oz.) can condensed cream of mushroom soup
- 1 1/3 cups milk

- 1/2 tsp. salt
- 1/4 tsp. freshly ground black pepper
- 1 cup dry bread crumbs
- 3 tbsps. melted butter
- 2 tsps. dried thyme, crushed

Direction

- Preheat the oven to 175 °C or 350 °F. Oil a 1-quart casserole dish.
- Boil a big pot of lightly salted water. Put in pasta and let cook till al dente for 8 to 10 minutes; drain.
- Put together pepper, salt, milk, and mushroom soup in a mixing bowl. Combine well. Then mix in pasta, mushrooms and tuna. Combine well. Into the greased casserole dish, put the mixture.
- Mix together thyme, butter and bread crumbs in a separate mixing bowl. Combine thoroughly. Scatter over tuna mixture.
- Without cover, bake in a prepped oven for 40 minutes till golden brown and bubbling.

Nutrition Information

- Calories: 298 calories;
- Total Carbohydrate: 30.7 g
- Cholesterol: 32 mg
- Total Fat: 11.5 g
- Protein: 18.3 g
- Sodium: 932 mg

191. Turkey Veggie Meatloaf Cups

""Here's my favorite delicious recipe! I gave this recipe mostly to my friends, and they love it too!""
Serving: 10 | Prep: 20m | Ready in: 50m

Ingredients

- 2 cups coarsely chopped zucchini
- 1 1/2 cups coarsely chopped onions
- 1 red bell pepper, coarsely chopped
- 1 lb. extra lean ground turkey
- 1/2 cup uncooked couscous

- 1 egg
- 2 tbsps. Worcestershire sauce
- 1 tbsp. Dijon mustard
- 1/2 cup barbecue sauce, or as needed

Direction

- Set the oven to 400°F (200°C) for preheating. Use a cooking spray to coat the 20 muffin cups.
- In a food processor, pulse the red bell pepper, zucchini, and onions several times until the ingredients are finely chopped but not liquefied. In a bowl, mix the vegetables, couscous, Dijon mustard, ground turkey, egg, and Worcestershire sauce until well-combined. Pour the mixture into the prepared muffin cups, filling each for about 3/4 full. Drizzle 1 tsp. of barbecue sauce into each of the cups.
- Allow them to bake inside the preheated oven for 25 minutes until all the juices run clear and the inserted instant-read meat thermometer registers at least 160°F (70°C). Allow them to stand for 5 minutes. Serve.

Nutrition Information

- Calories: 119 calories;
- Total Carbohydrate: 13.6 g
- Cholesterol: 47 mg
- Total Fat: 1 g
- Protein: 13.2 g
- Sodium: 244 mg

192. Vegan Mac And Cheese

"This recipe is sure to become your favorite!"
Serving: 8 | Prep: 5m | Ready in: 22m

Ingredients

- 1 1/2 (12 oz.) packages gluten-free elbow pasta
- 1 lb. butternut squash, peeled and cut into 1-inch pieces
- 1 1/2 cups soy milk
- 1 cup vegetable broth
- 1/2 tsp. salt

- 1/2 tsp. ground cayenne pepper
- 1/2 tsp. ground nutmeg
- 2 tbsps. chopped parsley, or to taste

Direction

- Boil the lightly salted water in a large pot. In boiling water, cook the gluten-free elbow macaroni for about 10 mins until tender but firm to bite, stirring occasionally. Drain.
- In a pot, combine vegetable broth, soymilk and butternut squash. Boil. Cook for about 12 mins until the squash becomes tender. Use an immersion blender to puree. Season with nutmeg, pepper and salt. Mix in the cooked macaroni. Decorate with the chopped parsley.

Nutrition Information

- Calories: 283 calories;
- Total Carbohydrate: 60.4 g
- Cholesterol: 0 mg
- Total Fat: 2.1 g
- Protein: 6.8 g
- Sodium: 229 mg

193. Vegan Portobello Stroganoff

"This is a new vegan version."
Serving: 4 | Prep: 10m | Ready in: 1h10m

Ingredients

- 8 oz. vegan sour cream (such as Tofutti®)
- 1/2 cup water
- 3 tbsps. dried minced onion
- 2 tbsps. all-purpose flour
- 2 tsps. vegan no-beef bouillon
- 1/4 tsp. garlic powder
- 1/4 tsp. dried basil
- 1/4 tsp. ground black pepper
- 1/2 cup dry red wine
- 1 tbsp. olive oil
- 2 tbsps. soy sauce
- 1 tbsp. balsamic vinegar
- 2 cloves garlic, minced

- 2 large portobello mushroom caps, stems and gills removed
- cooking spray
- 1/4 cup water, or as needed (optional)

Direction

- In a bowl, whisk black pepper, basil, garlic powder, vegan bouillon, flour, minced onion, half cup water and vegan sour cream. Refrigerate with a cover.
- Start preheating the oven to 400°F (200°C).
- In another bowl, whisk garlic, balsamic vinegar, soy sauce, olive oil and red wine.
- Place the mushroom caps in a baking dish with the gill sides up. Top with red wine mixture. Marinate for 20 mins, cover baking dish with the aluminum foil.
- Bake mushrooms for half an hour in preheated oven. Discard the foil, turn the mushrooms over. Keep baking about 10 more mins until very tender. Put aside to cool; then dice the mushrooms.
- Over medium heat, heat the saucepan sprayed with the cooking spray. Cook while stirring mushrooms in the saucepan for about 5 mins until browned lightly. Lower the heat to low.
- Stir the sour cream sauce into the mushrooms. Continue to cook while stirring for 1-2 more mins until thickened. Stir in a quarter cup of water if sauce is too thick.

Nutrition Information

- Calories: 259 calories;
- Total Carbohydrate: 25.9 g
- Cholesterol: 0 mg
- Total Fat: 13.5 g
- Protein: 3.3 g
- Sodium: 778 mg

194. Veggie Lo Mein

"Tasty!"
Serving: 6 | Prep: 15m | Ready in: 25m

Ingredients

- 1 lb. dry Chinese noodles
- 1 cup chopped fresh mushrooms
- 1 (8 oz.) can bamboo shoots, drained
- 1 cup chopped celery
- 1 cup bean sprouts
- 1/2 tsp. chopped garlic
- 1 tsp. salt
- 1 cup vegetable broth
- 1 tsp. white sugar
- 1 cup water
- 1 tbsp. soy sauce
- 1 tbsp. oyster sauce
- 1 tbsp. all-purpose flour

Direction

- Boil the lightly salted water in a large pot. Put in Chinese noodles. Cook for about 2-4 mins; then drain.
- In a wok or large skillet with a small amount of oil, cook garlic, bean sprouts, celery, bamboo shoots and mushrooms over high heat. Mix in oyster sauce, soy sauce, water, sugar, broth and salt, then stir. Put in flour. Cook until it is thickened. Pour over the noodles; lightly toss.

Nutrition Information

- Calories: 283 calories;
- Total Carbohydrate: 63.1 g
- Cholesterol: 0 mg
- Total Fat: 2 g
- Protein: 10.2 g
- Sodium: 713 mg

195. Verenika

"It's so luscious!"
Serving: 30 | Prep: 1h | Ready in: 1h30m

Ingredients

- 2 1/2 cups dry cottage cheese
- 2 eggs
- 1/4 tsp. ground black pepper to taste
- 3 3/4 cups all-purpose flour
- 1/3 cup nonfat dry milk powder
- 3/4 tsp. baking powder
- 1/2 tsp. salt
- 2 eggs
- 3/4 cup water
- 4 tsps. vegetable oil
- 3 tbsps. butter
- 1 cup cubed ham
- 3 tbsps. all-purpose flour
- 1/2 tsp. salt
- 1/8 tsp. black pepper
- 2 1/2 cups warm milk

Direction

- Combine ground black pepper to taste, two eggs and cottage cheese in a blender, covered, and blend until smooth, or using an electric mixer, beat until they become smooth. Put aside.
- Stir half tsp. of salt, baking powder, milk powder and flour together in a large bowl. Beat oil, water and 2 eggs together in a small bowl; mix with the flour mixture.
- Knead the dough on floured surface until they become smooth or about 10 times. Halve the dough, roll out per portion into a 1/8-inch-thick. Cut out rounds of the dough with a 4 inches round cutter.
- Place one tbsp. filling in the middle of every circle. Moisten edge. Form the half-moon shape by folding over; seal by pinching.
- Boil water in a large pot. Put in 1/2 dumplings. Cook until tender or for 8-10 mins. Using a slotted spoon, discard then drain. Do the same with the remaining dumplings.

- Prepare gravy as the dumplings cook. Melt butter in medium saucepan over medium-low heat. Mix in ham. Cook until the ham turns light brown. Put in 1/8 tsp. of the ground black pepper, half tsp. of salt and 3 tbsps. of the flour, then stir. Put in milk all at once, stirring constantly; cook while stirring until bubbly and thick. Pour over dumplings. Serve.

Nutrition Information

- Calories: 127 calories;
- Total Carbohydrate: 14.9 g
- Cholesterol: 35 mg
- Total Fat: 4.2 g
- Protein: 6.8 g
- Sodium: 254 mg

196. Yakisoba Chicken

"It's a yummy treat!"
Serving: 6 | Prep: 15m | Ready in: 30m

Ingredients

- 1/2 tsp. sesame oil
- 1 tbsp. canola oil
- 2 tbsps. chile paste
- 2 cloves garlic, chopped
- 4 skinless, boneless chicken breast halves - cut into 1 inch cubes
- 1/2 cup soy sauce
- 1 onion, sliced lengthwise into eighths
- 1/2 medium head cabbage, coarsely chopped
- 2 carrots, coarsely chopped
- 8 oz. soba noodles, cooked and drained

Direction

- Combine chili paste, canola oil and sesame oil in a large skillet; stir-fry for half a minute. Put in garlic. Stir fry 30 seconds more. Put in a quarter cup of the soy sauce and chicken. Stir fry for about 5 mins until chicken is no longer pink. Take off the mixture from the pan. Put aside, keep it warm.

- Combine carrots, cabbage, and onion in emptied pan. Stir-fry for 2-3 mins until the cabbage starts to wilt. Stir in chicken mixture, cooked noodles, and remaining soy sauce to pan; blend by mixing. Enjoy!

Nutrition Information

- Calories: 295 calories;
- Total Carbohydrate: 40.7 g
- Cholesterol: 46 mg
- Total Fat: 4.8 g
- Protein: 26.3 g
- Sodium: 1621 mg

197. Yves Veggie Heaven

"Great veggie pasta with green onion, ginger, garlic and Asian stir fry oil."
Serving: 4 | Prep: 5m | Ready in: 15m

Ingredients

- 2 tbsps. Spectrum® Asian Stir Fry Oil Organic
- 2 cloves garlic, diced
- 12 pearl onions
- 1 (340 gram) package Yves Veggie Cuisine® Original Veggie Ground Round
- 1/2 red pepper, julienned
- 1 small carrot, diced
- 1/2 cup Imagine® Organic Vegetable Broth
- 1 cup whole wheat rotini pasta
- steak seasoning to taste

Direction

- In a large skillet, heat oil.
- Stir in garlic; cook in 1 minute.
- Stir in onions; cook in 1 minute.
- Put in Yves Veggie Ground Round. Combine garlic and onions with Yves Veggie Ground Round.
- Stir in carrots and red pepper, toss until well-combined. Continue cooking for the flavors to meld in 1 minute.

- When everything is well-blended, add Imagine Broth and noodles in order.
- Stir and put cover on. Let it cook until the pasta reaches your desired texture, about 8 minutes.

Nutrition Information

- Calories: 273 calories;
- Total Carbohydrate: 30.9 g
- Cholesterol: 0 mg
- Total Fat: 9 g
- Protein: 18.5 g
- Sodium: 542 mg

198. Zaru Soba

"This Japanese soup is the best treat for those hot summer days."
Serving: 4 | Prep: 10m | Ready in: 50m

Ingredients

- 1 (8 oz.) package dried soba noodles
- 1 cup prepared dashi stock
- 1/4 cup soy sauce
- 2 tbsps. mirin
- 1/4 tsp. white sugar
- 2 tbsps. sesame seeds
- 1/2 cup chopped green onions
- 1 sheet nori (dried seaweed), cut into thin strips (optional)

Direction

- Boil the lightly salted water in pot. Put in soba noodles and cook for 5-8 mins until tender, stirring occasionally. Drain. Then, rinse under the cold water to speed up the cooling process.
- In small saucepan, combine white sugar, mirin, soy sauce and dashi. Boil. Take away from the heat. Let cool for about 25 mins to room temperature.
- Toss sesame seeds with noodles. Portion among four serving bowls. Spoon the dashi sauce over the noodles. Add nori and green onions on top.

Nutrition Information

- Calories: 257 calories;
- Total Carbohydrate: 48.2 g
- Cholesterol: < 1 mg
- Total Fat: 3.1 g
- Protein: 11.6 g
- Sodium: 1445 mg

199. Zoodle Lasagne

"This dish is still taste good the next day."
Serving: 4 | Prep: 20m | Ready in: 1h5m

Ingredients

- 4 zucchini
- 1 1/2 cups homemade or store-bought tomato sauce
- 2/3 cup shredded mozzarella cheese
- 1 1/2 cups bechamel sauce
- 1 cup grated Parmigiano Reggiano cheese
- 1/4 cup fresh basil, chopped

Direction

- Start preheating the oven to 375°F (190°C).
- Using a mandolin or knife, slice zucchini lengthwise into 1/4 inches in thickness.
- Pour 2 tbsps. of the tomato sauce onto bottom of 9x13 inches baking dish. Place the zucchini slices over the tomato sauce in single layer, slightly overlapping.
- Top with a thin mozzarella layer, one third bechamel, one third the remaining tomato sauce, one third Parmigiano Reggiano cheese and one third basil. Repeat these layers, add Parmigiano Reggiano cheese and bechamel for topping.
- Bake in preheated oven for about 35 mins until top turns golden brown and the sauce is bubbly. Let set for about 10 mins until the remaining liquid has absorbed.

Nutrition Information

- Calories: 281 calories;

- Total Carbohydrate: 15.5 g
- Cholesterol: 53 mg
- Total Fat: 18.1 g
- Protein: 16.2 g
- Sodium: 1778 mg

200. Zucchini Noodles And Summer Vegetables With Sweet Pepper Chicken Sausage

"Fresh veggies from the farmer's market and sweet pepper chicken sausage make this dish flavorful."
Serving: 4 | Prep: 15m | Ready in: 27m

Ingredients

- 2 zucchini, cut into noodle-shape strands
- 2 tbsps. extra-virgin olive oil, divided
- 1/2 cup chopped green bell pepper
- 1/3 cup chopped white onion
- 1 tbsp. seasoned salt (such as Spike® seasoning)
- 1 pinch sea salt and freshly ground black pepper to taste
- 2 sweet pepper chicken sausages, sliced
- 1 cup lightly torn fresh spinach
- 2 tbsps. chopped fresh basil
- 1 tsp. garlic paste
- 1 large tomato, diced
- 1/4 cup shredded Parmesan cheese

Direction

- In a pot, put water and a little salt; heat to a boil. To the boiling water, add zoodles or zucchini noodles and cook for 3 minutes until firm to chew but tender; drain water.
- In a frying pan, heat 1 tbsp. olive oil on medium; stir and cook onion, green bell pepper, sea salt, and seasoned salt, 3 minutes. Add the chicken sausage and cook for 4-5 minutes until sausage is light brown. Add the garlic paste, spinach, seasoned salt to taste, and basil; cook for 2-3 minutes until spinach wilts.
- Put zoodles on a platter and mix with sea salt and remaining 1 tbsp. olive oil. Add the sausage mixture and the tomatoes. Put Parmesan on top; use pepper and salt to season.

Nutrition Information

- Calories: 208 calories;
- Total Carbohydrate: 9.2 g
- Cholesterol: 40 mg
- Total Fat: 13.6 g
- Protein: 11.7 g
- Sodium: 1407 mg

Index

A

Allspice, 19

Almond, 13

Anchovies, 3, 37

Apple, 42

Arrowroot, 65

Artichoke, 4, 34, 75, 84

Asparagus, 3, 13, 29, 38, 74

Avocado, 15

B

Bacon, 53, 76, 78–80

Baking, 8, 13–14, 19, 23, 25–26, 33, 36, 40, 46–47, 49, 53–56, 60, 62, 64, 68–69, 71, 78, 81,

  85, 87, 92, 98, 101–102, 105, 107–108, 110

Baking powder, 78, 108

Balsamic vinegar, 17, 48, 83, 87, 107

Bamboo shoots, 21, 107–108

Barbecue sauce, 106

Basil, 3, 5, 8, 11–15, 17, 20, 24, 28, 31–32, 34–35, 38–39, 41, 43, 48, 50–52, 54–56, 65–66,

  68–69, 74, 77, 84–87, 91, 93–96, 101–103, 107, 110–111

Bay leaf, 37, 65

Beans, 4–5, 42–43, 49, 61–62, 67, 72, 84–85, 88–89, 93, 96–97

Beef, 3–4, 10, 15–16, 21, 23, 36, 38, 44–45, 49, 51–52, 58–60, 78–79, 81, 85–86, 92, 95, 107

Beef stock, 44

Black beans, 5, 88–89, 97

Black pepper, 8–9, 11, 14–15, 17–21, 26, 30–32, 34–35, 37, 39, 41–44, 46, 48–51, 53,

  56–57, 59, 62–63, 66, 68–74, 76–78, 82, 85–86, 89–91, 94–98, 100, 102–105, 107–108, 111

Bread, 10, 29, 57, 59, 64, 101, 104–106

Breadcrumbs, 60, 104

Brie, 5, 91

Broccoli, 3, 9–11, 29–30, 32, 35, 45, 74–75, 97

Broth, 9–11, 13, 16–17, 22, 32, 42, 45, 48, 50, 54, 59–61, 67–68, 70, 74–76, 82, 85, 92, 97,

  101–102, 104–109

Brown sugar, 33, 35

Brussels sprouts, 3, 18

Butter, 3, 12–13, 19, 22–23, 25–26, 29–31, 33, 35, 39, 41, 44–45, 48–50, 53, 57–61, 63,

  67–68, 73, 76, 78–81, 89–91, 98, 105–106, 108

Buttermilk, 57

Butternut squash, 3, 19, 106–107

C

Cabbage, 18, 21, 95–96, 109

Cake, 6

Cannellini beans, 72

Capers, 34, 37, 55, 94–95, 104

M

Macaroni, 3–4, 23, 30–31, 33, 40, 45, 49, 57, 61–64, 66, 72, 82–83, 88, 107

Margarine, 30, 49, 57, 82, 89

Marjoram, 39, 47

Matzo, 4, 71

Mayonnaise, 28–29

Meat, 4, 9, 15–16, 43–45, 49, 58–59, 67, 69, 88, 92, 101, 106

Milk, 9, 12–13, 16, 29–31, 39–40, 45, 47, 50, 53–54, 57–58, 61, 79–80, 82, 85, 90, 105–106,

   108

Mint, 16, 57–60, 85

Mirin, 51, 110

Mozzarella, 8–9, 12, 14, 20, 24, 26, 29–30, 36, 40, 44, 47–48, 51–52, 54–56, 66, 71, 77,

   85–86, 92–93, 103–104, 110

Muffins, 4, 52

Mushroom, 3–5, 9, 14, 16–17, 20, 24–29, 31, 35–37, 40, 43–45, 48–49, 53–56, 60–61,

   65–66, 68–70, 75–79, 81, 84–85, 87, 95–97, 100–101, 103, 105–108

Mustard, 44–45, 57, 81, 100–102, 106

N

Noodles, 3–6, 10, 19, 21, 24, 26–33, 35–36, 40, 44–45, 49, 51–56, 63–64, 66, 68–70, 75–76,

   85–86, 90–93, 95–96, 98–99, 105, 107–111

Nori, 110

Nut, 38, 43, 101

Nutmeg, 19, 23, 50, 82, 99, 106–107

O

Oil, 4, 8–13, 16–18, 20–22, 24–28, 32–35, 37–38, 40–41, 43, 46–49, 51, 53–56, 58–62, 65–76,

   78, 80–84, 86–93, 95–104, 106–109, 111

Olive, 4, 8, 10–11, 14, 16–18, 20–22, 24–28, 34, 37–38, 40–43, 46–49, 51, 54–56, 58–62,

   65–68, 71–78, 82–84, 86–91, 93, 97–98, 100–104, 107, 111

Olive oil, 8, 10–11, 16–18, 20–22, 24, 27–28, 34, 37–38, 40–41, 43, 46–48, 51, 54–56,

   58–62, 65–68, 71–76, 78, 82–84, 86–91, 93, 97–98, 100–104, 107, 111

Onion, 4, 8–11, 14, 16–18, 20–37, 41, 44–46, 49–51, 53–55, 59–62, 64–70, 72, 74–83, 88,

   90–93, 95–99, 104, 106–107, 109–111

Orange, 45–46, 48, 75

Orange juice, 75

Oregano, 8, 13, 17, 33, 37, 42–43, 48, 54–56, 65–66, 69, 77, 84, 86, 93–95

Oyster, 35, 92, 108

Oyster sauce, 35, 92, 108

P

Pancakes, 4, 58

Pancetta, 4, 76

Paprika, 35, 38, 58–59, 63

Parmesan, 3, 6, 9, 11, 13–17, 19–21, 24–25, 30, 32–33, 37–39, 41–44, 48–49, 51–52, 54,

   56, 59–61, 66, 68, 71–78, 82–83, 85–89, 92–94, 97,

Conclusion

Thank you again for downloading this book!

I hope you enjoyed reading about my book!

If you enjoyed this book, please take the time to share your thoughts and post a review on Amazon. It'd be greatly appreciated!

Write me an honest review about the book – I truly value your opinion and thoughts and I will incorporate them into my next book, which is already underway.

Thank you!

If you have any questions, **feel free to contact at:** _mspasta@mrandmscooking.com_

Ms. Pasta

www.MrandMsCooking.com

Printed in the USA
CPSIA information can be obtained
at www.ICGtesting.com
LVHW070000041223
765600LV00055B/2209